The Arthur Ranch on East Divide Creek

Memories of western Colorado in the 1960s and 70s

Kathleen Arthur

Printed in the United States of America
ISBN: 978-1483963464

To my mom, Betty Arthur, whose passion for the stories inspired me to keep writing.

To my love, Lee Smith, who added creative perspective and lots of patience.

And to Tammi Whitaker, my sister, my playmate, my "partner in crime" and my friend.

For my kids, Matt and Piper.

CONTENTS

The Ranch   1

The ranch was south of Silt, Colorado on East Divide Creek. In the 1960s and 70s, we were really out in the boondocks. Except Sadie Connors, the hermit who lived another 15 miles on up in the mountains, we were the last place up the creek where people lived year-round. Garfield County graded the road in the spring and graveled it every few years. In winter, the snowplow turned around at our gate and only plowed when the snow got too deep for our four wheel drive pickup. We lived at the end of the mail route. The mail lady, Mrs. Bair, came twice a week.

It's not clear to me how the Arthur ranch was put together or who homesteaded which parts that eventually became our ranch. The ranch, as we knew it, was 984 acres. Often the bigger places were put together by buying smaller places from the homesteaders or early owners. My great great Uncle Hamilton (Ham) Arthur got the place in 1902. He and his family lived in the old cabin while he built the two story house Grandma and Grandad Arthur lived in when I was growing up. One of the Bottorfs may have had something to do with homesteading the place.

In 1947, Uncle Ham sold the ranch to his nephew, my grandad Arthur. Loren and Mary Arthur and their two boys, Steve and Jack moved from California to the ranch. My father, Jack, was the younger of the two. I'm not sure when or why they went to California. My father was born in Fairplay in 1933 and my grandfather was born in Cripple Creek in 1899. The Arthurs had a long history of ranching, working in the gold mines and banking in and around Fairplay and Cripple Creek. By the 1930s, gold mining around Cripple Creek was not as profitable as it had once been. As a blacksmith at the South London gold mine, perhaps Grandad thought he would do better providing for his family by hiring on at one of the big hay ranches in California. Sometime after they bought the ranch in 1947, Grandad bought the Moore place, 200 acres located seven or eight miles above the ranch. That was our high country summer pasture for the cows.

My father worked on various oil rigs in Colorado and Utah, and the molybdenum mine at Climax for a short while when he got back from the Navy in 1957. He returned to the ranch in a few years to help Grandma and Grandad take care of the place, bringing with him his young wife and two daughters. Mom, Betty Jo [Cole] Arthur was called Betty Jo but many people called her Betty and Daddy sometimes called her Bet. When she married Daddy, Mom was a town girl. She'd grown up frugally so that aspect of life she could deal with. But she must have really loved the guy to follow my dad to a cabin way out in the country with an outhouse and where much of her time would be spent getting firewood and carrying coal and water to the house.

I was a toddler and my sister, Tammi Jo was barely walking. In 1960, Grandad added to the ranch by buying the Jayne place of about 200 acres from Lee Smith so we had a place to live. In 1961, Mom, Daddy and we two girls moved into the cabin. I always called it our house. A cabin is where people went to vacation or camp out. Our house is where we lived, regardless of what it looked like. The Jones place was between our house and Grandma and Grandad's.

There must have been a King place and a Heatherly place because the two ditches on our ranch were called the King ditch and the really big one was the King-Heatherly ditch. Those ditches didn't service any ranch but ours although a few shares of water did belong to the Hall place directly down the creek from our ranch. They were both very long ditches to send water to our more distant hayfields. Mom and I remember a Heatherly place but it was on up East Divide Creek, between our ranch and the upper pasture.

Down the creek from Grandma and Grandad's gate, in a pasture sharing a fence line with one of our hayfields was the site of the town of Raven, Colorado. There weren't any ruins of the town left but my dad and grandparents pointed out the location many times when I was a girl. Raven had a post office from 1898 to 1939 and there was a stage line between New Castle and Raven. Down the road about a mile was our school bus stop and the remains of the Raven school. The rock foundation still exists. Daddy called it the Larsen School.

The 984 acres of our ranch was about 450 acres of hayfields, and the rest in hillsides, pastures, gullies and creek bottom. Most of the hayfields were on the west side of the creek. East Divide Creek isn't much as creeks go, but the ranch's very existence depended on it. In the spring, it's a raging torrent, promising destruction to everything in its path. In a couple of weeks, when high water from the mountain snow melt is over, the creek settles down to a lazy, meandering stream. By mid-August, it's almost dry. The county road more or less follows the creek. The Arthur place started a few hundred yards below Grandma and Grandad's driveway and continued until about a quarter of a mile above our driveway, about 2 miles all together.

The creek called to me. From the time I was a toddler, I climbed under, over or through any fence they devised to keep me corralled and wasn't discouraged by sound slaps on my diapered little behind. I suppose it was sheer good luck and our mother's eagle eye that kept me from falling in the creek and drowning, dragging my little sister along with me.

The valley the ranch occupied was in the mountains south of and several hundred feet higher in elevation than the Colorado River. The headwaters of East Divide Creek are at Reservoir Park, it joins West Divide just below the ranch and runs into the Colorado River near the town of Silt.

People often associate up with north and down with south. Our geography and terrain south of the Colorado

River was just the opposite. Visitors got turned around in the mountains, forgetting that going further up into the mountains was actually going south. We spent so much time up in those mountains there was never a worry any of us, even when we kids were quite young, would get lost. Put any of us in a town or city bigger than Rifle or Glenwood and that's a whole different story. The mountains south of the ranch where we spent so much time was mostly the White River National Forest and BLM (Bureau of Land Management), with some small tracts of private acreage like our upper pasture interspersed. We simply called it all the high country or said we were going up-country.

The ranch was fenced on the west side of the road where hayfields and pastures dipped towards the creek bottom. There were ditches at the top of each field for irrigating. If the field was very big, there was another feeder ditch cutting across the middle of the field. It was all about water management when we were irrigating, getting about the same amount of water to every part of every hayfield and pasture if possible.

Piles of rocks were stacked near the fence every now and then. It was an unspoken rule that anyone walking across a hayfield picked up any rocks they found and threw them up by the fence. No matter how many rocks we picked up, there were always more. If we complained about having to pick up rocks, Mom usually said, "Well, we do live in the Rocky Mountains." Rocks in the hayfield played havoc with farm machinery.

When we talked about the rocks around our place, we generally used sandstone and lava rock to generically describe all the rocks. I imagine most people would use the word granite instead of lava because that's what it was. There was quartz, different schists and other metamorphic rock. The geologic make up of our part of the country on the western slope of the Rocky Mountains was mostly igneous and metamorphic. But we were also at the very eastern edge of an ancient sea that had covered much of the western United States so we had sedimentary rock including coal and oil shale from the swamps near the edge of the ancient sea.

Our whole family loved to look for, look at and bring home rocks. Rocks, rocks and more rocks. We had rocks of all shapes, colors and sizes. None of them were valuable to anyone but us but they were always odd, pretty or unusual in some way. One of the most interesting was something Daddy called conglomerate. It was made of all sorts of small, different colored rocks that had been worn smooth by the creek tumbling them around. Then they were all stuck together into a big rock by sand and small bits of gravel that had somehow made a natural cement. Very neat. There was also petrified wood and a semi-precious stone called jasper, and it was a real find if you discovered any.

The east side of the county road going through our ranch was not fenced and was cedar and sagebrush hillside. Halfway between the lower place, where my grandparents lived, and our place was the Jones place. Just off the road at the Jones place were the remains of a dwelling, near an apricot tree. Mom said it was more of a dugout than a cabin. We poked around the ruins once in a while and found bits of colored glass. Usually when we were playing, the Jones place was someplace we passed through on our way to or from somewhere else rather than stopping to play.

Apricot trees were prevalent in our country. I imagine pioneers planted apricots because they were easy to grow, didn't take much water and could be eaten fresh, canned, dried, in cobblers and pies or as jam and jelly. It is the all around perfect fruit. Sometimes you'll see an apricot tree on a ditch bank or hillside where you know no human planted it. Squirrels, birds and chipmunks might plant the seeds without knowing it as they went about their business of collecting food for the winter.

Past the ruins of the dugout and the apricot tree, a dirt track went down a hill, around a corner and across a wooden bridge over East Divide Creek up to the hayfields. The road went straight up the hill, directly through the hayfield past the orchard. At the crest of the hill, it crossed the King Heatherly ditch and went through the hayfields down to the gully. There were hayfields on the other side of the gully but no permanent road. The only driving we did over there was with the swather and tractors during haying season. All of these hayfields were on very steep, sidling hillside. Next to the gully was the stack yard for all the hay from the Jones' place.

Ranching, especially a family operation, has never been a money making proposition but it was the way my parents and grandparents made their living. Pay day came once a year, when the calves were sold in the fall. There wasn't a salary involved for my folks and sometimes I imagine we were living more on love and hope than cash. While we were on the ranch (about fourteen years), the time my folks spent doing the work wasn't given any value. They didn't get a wage and Mom had to ask Grandad when she needed money for groceries.

I knew a lot of my friends had parents that went to work every day and had weekends off. Having my parents and grandparents around and available twenty four hours a day, seven days a week was normal for us. So the way the other kids lived seemed to be the oddity and we felt sorry for them. My folks didn't go to work but they were always working. Ranching, especially taking care of the animals, knew no holidays, weekends or vacations. They worked hard but when they took a few hours off, my folks played hard too. We spent many happy days camping, picnicking, fishing, plinking away at tin cans with the .22 rifle and generally romping around in the high country.

There were three orchards on the ranch. All of them had fruit trees planted in straight lines, the orchard carefully planned to take advantage of waste water from irrigating nearby hayfields and pastures. The orchards were big enough that there would have been more apples, pears, apricots and plums than one family could handle so maybe at one time they sold some of the fruit. I don't know. None of the orchards had been attended to in many years in terms of pruning, spraying for insects, etc. So many of the trees never produced much for us except enough to snag an apple or some apricots for a snack as we ran and played. As with many things, we kids didn't pay much attention to the orchards. They did provide good shade on a hot summer day and a place to sit down under a tree and take a break.

The orchard at our place was very close to the house but much older than our house. So the Jayne family must have had another house somewhere nearby. There were no more than five or six trees in our orchard and I think they were all apple trees.

The biggest of the three orchards was at the Jones place, maybe twenty trees or so. The orchard was a long way from the dugout down by the creek so it made me wonder if there hadn't been a cabin closer to the orchard at one time.

The third orchard made up Grandma and Grandad's backyard. It got more water than the others so we got more fruit from those trees. Some years, the pear tree next to the clothesline was loaded and we got lots of pears to eat. There was an Italian plum tree. The plums were sour if you tried to eat them too soon but if you waited for the first frost, they were very sweet. Across the backyard orchard, on the path headed for the spring house was a sugar plum tree. It was a big producer and Mom made lots of yummy plum jelly.

Herefords and Holsteins   2

We ran about 100 head of mother cows with two bulls on our ranch. We only ran Herefords, or red white faces as we called them. This was long before so much cross breeding was done to create more meat faster. Our family thought Herefords were hardy, easy keepers and produced well. They weren't prone to disease or temperament and didn't grow to be huge, muscle bound animals. Hereford cows, after their first calf, had few issues carrying a calf each year, calving in the spring and producing a nice healthy calf.

Putting up the hay and taking care of our small herd of cattle, the horses, milk cows and a few other animals kept my parents and grandparents busy all day every day. We weren't a big enough operation to warrant hired help so during irrigation and haying season, it was all my family could do to handle everything that needed to be done.

Contrary to popular belief, cattle ranchers and their families don't eat much beef. Selling the steers in the fall was our only source of income, so every steer on a family run operation like ours needed to be sold. We had pigs on the ranch and usually butchered at least one each year. We had hams and bacon cured at the locker plant in town. We also had pork roast, sausage, sidemeat (uncured bacon) and lots of pork chops. Mom bought our hamburger at the store. We grew up eating venison along with trout, chicken, pork and hamburger. Daddy also got at least one elk and one deer during hunting season for us to cut up, package and freeze. We always had a deer in the freezer or one hanging in the shed. During the year, even when it wasn't hunting season, Daddy got us a deer whenever we needed meat. We called it farmer's season and the local game wardens looked the other way though they knew full well what was going on.

In the late summer after we brought the cows down from the pasture up-country and in the winter, we let them have the run of the place leaving all the gates open between pastures and fields. When we started irrigating and the alfalfa and grasses began to grow in the hayfields, those gates were shut. Obviously, we needed to put up the hay to use for feed in the winter. Also, if cows eat too much green alfalfa, it can make them very sick. It doesn't affect horses that way.

Tammi and I spent a lot of time playing, walking and running around in pastures, hayfields and high mountain meadows. I imagine most of it was for fun but sometimes we were trying to head off a cow, catch a horse or kick a calf out of the brush. Sometimes I think Daddy sent us off across a pasture on some made-up reason just to get us out of his hair for awhile.

There were several hazards in running across any field on or near a cattle ranch. Besides various stickers, burrs and thistles, there was the manure. Call it what you want, cow pies, cow patties, it's still wet, sticky and smelly when the cow first drops it "splat" on the road or in the field. If there was fresh cow manure anywhere in the county, I was going to step in it. And I knew it when it happened, always a split second after I could have avoided the disaster. If we were wearing our boots, it was mostly just annoying. A little time standing on one leg like a stork with a nice little stick in hand, you could scrape most of the muck off your boot and then scuff the rest off in the dust and dirt. If you were wearing your Keds, or some other low-topped shoe, you might not fare so well. Nothing like gooey, sticky, smelly, ugly green and yellow cow manure running over the top and down into your shoe. Give it a day and the cow patty in the pasture dried up. Then it wasn't so bad.

We were always doing something with the cattle. If we weren't moving them from one place to another, we were checking on them, looking for injuries or illness. We made sure they had salt blocks and access to fresh water and feed. We helped them calve, fed hay in the winter, branded, castrated and dehorned the bull calves, and put the momma cows with the bulls to breed. All year long there was something to be done with the cows.

Although we branded and ear-tagged our cattle, we didn't keep track of and log information about each individual cow like they do now. Grandad kept a ranch journal which was mostly counts of cows, new calves, bales of hay and the day's low and high temperatures. We did do a rough count every time we gathered or moved the cows. It was an important job and though an adult generally did the counting, they often enlisted one of us to do a count as well. Someone else tried to keep the gate almost closed so only one or two cows went through at a time for easier counting. But sometimes the pushing and shoving cows would be too much for the gate keeper and several would push through at one time. That's when a second person taking count helped.

Across the lane from Grandma and Grandad's house was the calf pasture. It had barbed wire fences but unlike most of the ranch, it had a wooden gate just wide enough to walk through or lead a cow through. The milk cows, orphaned or sick calves, or any other animals that needed to be kept in were put in the calf pasture. The calf pasture didn't have any water, except in the ditch during irrigating, so there was a metal water tank inside the fence, near the gate. Grandad had enough hoses so we could fill the water tank with water from the house. At our house, if we had any animals in the corral or other pens, water had to be hauled in buckets from the creek.

There was a pasture on the creek and near Grandma and Grandad's house that we called the sawmill. Not only did we keep the milk cows there some of the time, we also had a big stack yard and parked a lot of the farm machinery there. Beyond the sawmill was a gate into a very large hayfield that we called the Thirteen Acres. It produced well every year so the haystack out in the sawmill was often one of the biggest on the ranch.

≈

We had around a dozen Holstein cows for milking. Holsteins were bigger and much taller than our Herefords and were spotted, black and white. We bred our milk cows to our Hereford bulls. The calves were let suck once a day and the mama didn't give as much milk at milking time. When they were old enough to drink skim milk out of a bucket, they were taken away from their mother so she could produce more milk for us.

Until we built the cabin at the Moore place, the barn in the barnyard at Grandma and Grandad's house was the newest building on the ranch, finished in 1952. It was made completely out of cinder blocks with a cement floor so was always cool and downright cold in the winter. My grandparents had run a little dairy on the ranch before I was born so they had fancy automated milking machines and a cream separator. The milk room was where the parts of the milking machines were stored between milkings and where the cream separator was. If we had orphaned calves, we bottle fed them with a supplement called milk replacer until they were old enough to drink milk out of a bucket. The milk replacer came in powdered form and Grandma kept the bags in the milk room.

Outside the door to the milk room was a steep, rocky hill that went up and around to the front door of Grandma and Grandad's house. No one drove up or down that hill except with a tractor once in awhile. When farm machinery broke down, they took it to the barn where the tools were for repairs but they usually came down on the other side of the barnyard where it wasn't as steep or rocky.

The granary was a sturdy two story wooden building with a good plank floor. It was built so the back part of the building was rocked up with a partial foundation. Rather than level the hill out for the granary they put the front of the building on stilts so the floor was level. I'm not sure why it wasn't used. My guess is that previous generations bought feed in larger amounts than we did because going to town, even Silt which was only ten miles away, was an all day trip. It was easy enough for us to go to town to get feed at the Co-op eight or ten bags at a time. We played in the granary but not very often. Mom found several nice clean, not rusty, metal cans in the rafters one time. I think she still uses one of them for her embroidery thread.

Each morning, the cows were brought from the sawmill, barnyard or calf pasture to the corral outside the barn. In the evening, the cows weren't turned out in the pasture but were kept in the corral by the barn overnight so they'd be readily available for the next morning's milking. The barn had a large sliding door on the west side leading directly into the corral. I think we milked three or four cows at a time. They were brought into the barn where each cow had its own stanchion which kept her from backing out of the stall while still connected to the milking machine. The stanchion allowed the cows to lift and lower their heads so they could eat hay while they were being milked. They also had a set of hobbles on their hind legs because milk cows, ours anyway, were known to kick from time to time.

Our milk cows were tame enough Grandad could pretty much walk each cow into the barn, right into the stall, close the stanchion and put on the hobbles. Of course, the fact that there was fresh hay in the feed bins in front of each stanchion didn't hurt. I'm sure some or all of the milk cows had names but I don't remember any of them. I know they were all called "SOB" at one time or another.

Each cow had her own personality. One of ours was especially prone to kicking. We all stood clear of her. We were careful to stay out of the way when they were being put in and out of the barn. When a milk cow steps on your foot, she kinda just stands there and takes her own sweet time picking up her foot again. That night it was time to soak your poor, swollen foot in Epsom salts. If you could get your boot off, that is. At least one of the cows would wait until they were in the barn to lift her tail and drop a nice sloppy cow pie on Grandad's nice clean cement floor. We thought it was funny but I don't think Grandad found it all that amusing. Grandad said she waited all day to do it.

Before putting the cows in the barn, Grandad and Grandma got all the parts of the clean milking machines from the milk room. They assembled the hoses and stainless steel parts and put them in a rack above where the cows would stand. Grandad had a short, three legged stool he carried from cow to cow to connect them up to the milking machine.

The machine fit over the cow's udder with a rubber tube over each teat. The machine simulated the action of hand milking and as the milk came, each tube sucked up the milk into a three or four gallon container that was part of the machine at each stanchion. Grandad spent time talking to each cow and rubbing their udder until the milk came. If a cow just wouldn't let her milk down, Grandad pulled off the machine and milked her by hand until the milk came. Then the machine was re-attached. When the cow was done milking, the machine was removed and Grandad finished milking her by hand. This was called stripping the teat and it was important to keep the cow healthy to produce milk for the next milking.

If there were enough cows, when one was finished milking, she'd be put back in the corral and another one brought in. If any of the cow's teats or udders (we called them bags) got chapped and sore, Grandma and Grandad had plenty of bag balm on hand and applied it liberally as needed. Bag balm is great for healing chapped and cracking skin on humans too.

As each cow finished giving milk, Grandad hauled the containers of milk into the milk room where Grandma ran it through the cream separator. After the cream was separated from the milk, it was put in metal cream cans and sold to the Glenwood Springs Creamery. Sometimes we took it to town. Sometimes the mail lady picked it up. I don't remember much about selling the cream. We stopped doing that when I was very young because Grandma and Grandad milked fewer cows and our two families used the milk and cream we got. Extra milk was fed to the barn cats, orphaned calves and to slop the hogs. People and animals alike loved that milk.

Milk cows got preferential treatment over that of the beef cows. Holsteins could live well into their twenties and produce milk much of that time. While they were being milked, besides hay the milk cows got a nutritional supplement that came in small pellet form. They ate those pellets like they were candy. When we brought the pellets home from the feed store, the bag was opened and the pellets dumped into a barrel with a tight lid. Even so, we sometimes found a mouse in the barrel. We never figured out how they could get in but they couldn't get out. Once we found a nest of baby mice in the barrel. We were quite upset when Grandad went to get rid of them even though we knew it had to be done.

There weren't many mice in the barn because Grandma had so many barn cats. They all knew when it was milking time and gathered outside the barn door where she put down pans of fresh, warm milk for them. The barn cats were feral and wild for the most part so we left them alone. Once in awhile one would be friendly enough to pet and be given a name. Some years, feline distemper would decimate the population. Fortunately, the house cats didn't interact much with the barn cats so they didn't get sick. Otherwise, natural predators also helped keep the barn cat numbers down.

Every morning and every night, every day of the year, the cows had to be milked and the milking machines and separator thoroughly cleaned. My grandparents didn't miss a milking except once in a blue moon, then Dad had to do it. Rain or shine, sick or well, the cows had to be milked. There was no calling in sick with this job. Not only could you not miss a single milking, it was best to not be late or early. Cows produce more milk if they are milked at the same time every morning and evening. A good producer could give three gallons of milk, twice a day. After the milking while Grandma took the milking machines and separator apart, Grandad shoveled out the barn. He had a scoop shovel he used just for that purpose, tossing the shovel full of manure and hay leaves out the big side door of the barn, into the corral.

Besides the pile of manure in the corral, there was also a big pile of older manure in the middle of the barnyard. Aged cow manure is great fertilizer so in the spring, Mom shoveled a pickup full from the older mound and spread it on our garden and flower beds. As manure ages, it breaks up into an organic matter much like dirt and is really not unpleasant to touch or smell at all. For hayfields where the cows hadn't wintered, we took manure from the barnyard to fertilize the alfalfa. A manure spreader is a piece of farm equipment that looks somewhat like a wagon and is pulled by a tractor. As the tractor moves across the field, the manure is augered out the bottom of the spreader.

One thing I learned from my grandparents was those milking machines could never be too clean after each milking. There was no running water in the barn. Grandma and Grandad carried buckets of hot and cold water from the house when they went down to the barn to milk. After milking, each milking machine was dunked down into a bucket of hot water and Clorox. The water also got sucked up into the storage container. Then everything was rinsed in cold water. After the cream separator was broken down into its component parts, everything was hauled to the house, given a thorough cleaning and then lugged back down to the barn, ready for the next milking. Grandma had a routine to it and she never varied.

The milk was put in gallon glass jars for us to take home. We picked up several gallons of milk whenever we went to the lower place (Grandma and Grandad's) to get water. We bought our mayonnaise in gallon glass jars so they became milk jars. Also, when Mom was young, coffee was sold in square gallon glass jars and we had several of those. Besides the one we used for milk, one of the coffee jars was our cookie jar. Another held dry pinto beans. Another had brown sugar, etc.

The whole milk was used to fill our milk jars for drinking before running it through the separator after which you got cream and skim milk. From experience, Mom learned some jars had lids that didn't stay screwed on tight during the trip to our house so she put a piece of waxed paper over the jar and under the lid. As it sat in the jar, the milk separated again and there was always a thick layer of cream at the top of each jar. We skimmed off some of it to use on cereal and stirred the rest back into the milk for drinking. It was the best tasting milk and the sweetest cream I've ever had.

Sometimes we made homemade butter from the ranch cream. Our churn was a square coffee jar. The outside of the lid had a handle and the inside of the lid had some sort of geared contraption that churned the cream. It took a lot of time, patience and persistence turning that handle to make butter. It was kind of the same idea as the homemade ice cream bucket we had but you didn't have to turn the handle for as long to make ice cream as you did to make butter. Fresh farm cream made really tasty homemade ice cream and butter.

Doing the Chores 3

In my world, there were town kids and country kids. Our town friends either went to the same school we did or rode our school bus. So we saw each other every day. We'd also see them at special events like the County Fair. Otherwise it seemed to me like they pretty much stayed in town. Once in awhile, we passed a vehicle with a schoolmate in it on the county road near our house. I imagined they were dragged away from whatever town kids did by their well meaning parents for a family weekend afternoon outing in the country. They would be headed back to town and home before dark.

Ranch kids, to be honest, were a bit snooty about our way of life over that of those poor kids who had to live in town. My Mom still laughs about one of the first times my sister or I spent the night with a town friend. When we came home, we complained there simply wasn't anything to do in town. Sometimes we went to a movie at the theater in Rifle, or bought sodas and candy at the drugstore, but that didn't happen often because we usually had no cash. Breakfast was one of those cereals we saw advertised like Trix or Captain Crunch. Which was fun. But that was pretty much it. I thought it was so rude when my friends took a phone call from another friend and talked for what I thought was a long time, basically ignoring me. I guess they spent the night with each other more often than we did and it wasn't as much of a big deal with them. And they were used to having a phone, which I wasn't.

With several of my friends, it seemed like their family never did sit down to eat together. I thought that was weird. I guess the parents were at meetings, or at least out. The food was also strange, supper was often one thing and out of a can, like Chef Boy R Dee Spaghetti-Os. I was used to dinner and supper both being a full meal: meat, potatoes, vegetables, salad, bread and dessert. Our midday meal was the biggest meal of the day because everyone had put in several hours of work by then. So we ate a big meal and usually took a break of a half hour or so. With that twinkle in his eye, Dad called it our siesta. We never called the noon meal lunch. It was always dinner. And in the evening we didn't have dinner, we had supper. So our meals were breakfast, dinner and supper.

Likewise, town kids didn't do so well spending the night with us. There was no television, no telephone and no corner drug store to walk to for candy or gum. We played cards, board games and let's pretend. We brushed our teeth and rinsed the toothbrush using a glass of water rather than running water in the sink. We didn't have central heating so in winter the sheets were flannel and linoleum floors in the morning were cold on bare feet. We drank unprocessed milk and ate unprocessed eggs, venison and home canned fruit and vegetables. We also had tasty homemade bread but some of our town friends didn't like it for toast or sandwiches. I guess they preferred Wonder bread.

The only time we ranch kids ever claimed to be scared of the dark was when we had overnight town company. If the guest had to go to the outhouse after dark or in the middle of the night, we went with them. By the time we left the house, our friend had told so many what-if stories we were convinced there were critters waiting in the dark to do bad things to little girls. When we didn't have town friends with us, we knew there was nothing to be scared of and it wasn't all that dark anyway because we always had flashlights. Of course, Mom and Dad didn't buy the scared bit for a second.

One of the things I didn't like about spending the night in town was it was never really dark and it was never really quiet. There were always streetlights, night lights and traffic noise. At our house, when it was dark and quiet, it was definitely dark and quiet. It always seemed so peaceful on the ranch and so hectic in town. I guess it all depends on what you get used to.

≈

Members of my family were not very superstitious, but we had a lot of fun with such things. Mom and Dad told stories of their grandparents and great aunts and uncles actually believing in some superstitions such as:

- Step on a crack, break your mother's back (for sidewalks and floor tile).

- It's bad luck if a black cat walks across in front of you or if you walk under a ladder (which kind of makes sense).
- If you break a mirror, you'll have seven years bad luck.
- If you spill salt, throw some over your left shoulder so you won't have bad luck.
- If you get a quick shiver when it's not cold, someone is walking on your grave.
- If you have an itchy nose, company is coming.

We had lots of other sayings or truisms. Just because they are clichés doesn't make them any less valid – or funny. We said such things as:

- Don't tell anyone you saw something in the newspaper, you'll never find it again.
- A watched pot never boils.
- If you want something done, ask a busy person.
- He must be tied to his mother's apron strings.
- It's six of one, half a dozen of the other.
- Sounds like you're between a rock and a hard place.
- If the beaver are building lots of dams, they're saving water. It will be a dry year next year.
- For an unsolicited opinion or advice: that and a dime will buy you a cup of coffee.
- Shake a leg, we're burnin' daylight.

Both Dad and Grandad liked to call anyone who wasn't driving to their satisfaction a flatlander. Usually this meant we were on a narrow, mountain road and the car in front of us was going too slow. Other favorites for other drivers were:

- He's taking his half out of the middle.
- He has nowhere to go and all day to get there.
- He was going down the road like a bat out of hell.
- He has a lead foot.

Dad had favorite sayings and beliefs related to we kids. To discourage us from asking for coffee, he said:

- Coffee will make your hair curl.
- Coffee will put hair on your chest.
- If you're old enough to drink coffee, you're old enough to drink it hot and black.

When we started driving, Daddy teased us:

- Keep the flaps down. (Don't drive too fast).
- Try and keep it between the hedges. (Don't run off the road).

And, of course, there were always these:

- If you're old enough to catch a fish, you're old enough to clean it.
- If you're old enough to shoot a deer, you're old enough to gut it out and get it back to the house.

$$\approx$$

By the 1960s, most people in the United States had electric or gas heat, hot water and indoor plumbing. We were the only family I knew who didn't have running water in the house and an outhouse around back. But since that was the way it was, it didn't seem unusual to us. About a mile up the road from Grandma and Grandad's place was our house. The lane started at the county road, went past the corrals, tack shed, headgate to the King ditch, chicken shed and woodshed, over the bridge and up the hill to the house. The house was tucked under a bunch of tall locust trees. We didn't have water to grow a lawn so our front and back yards were weeds, wild grasses and what lilac bushes and hollyhocks, petunias and marigolds Mom could grow by watering them with the dishwater. Our house was a small log cabin. It had a kitchen, living room, cellar (under the kitchen floor), pantry and two tiny bedrooms separated by a closet. There was a big fireplace and chimney made of river rock and a path to the outhouse that went around back. Mom said we had "four rooms and a path."

We hauled our drinking water in 2 ten gallon metal milk cans from Grandma and Grandad's house. Their water came from a spring that was near East Divide Creek, through the orchard behind their house. The spring and how it was pumped to Grandma and Grandad's house was a mystery to me. The kids were all warned to stay away from the spring house. We didn't want to know what the or else was so we stayed away. I imagine they just wanted to keep the water supply intact and clean.

The full water cans were heavy, with a sturdy handle on each side. It took two adults to carry the water, lift it into the pickup, then at home get the cans out of the pickup and haul them up to the house. Later, someone found a little metal cart that was made for moving milk cans. It looked like any other hand truck or dolly but was smaller and had a hook to hold the handle. That way our water cans could be moved around by one person. Since it was such a chore to get the water, we were very careful not to waste it.

Our water cans sat on the porch just outside the kitchen door. Our front porch had a rock and dirt floor and was cool, even in summer. The water was ice cold when we put it in the can because it came out of a spring cold, clear and tasting great. The heavy metal can kept the water cold. We had a large metal ladle with the handle bent over into the shape of a hook that hung on the side of the water can. Whenever we wanted a drink of water, we used the water dipper, got a drink out of the can, and put the water dipper back.

We actually did have running cold water in the sink in the kitchen but I don't remember much about it. It drained out through a pipe in the kitchen wall or floor, across the few feet of our side yard, then through the fence into the garden spot. Mom hardly ever turned the water on because it couldn't be used for anything. The water was from a well in the front yard, and it smelled strongly of sulphur. It also had a blackish/brackish color. Dad said the well was probably drilled into a coal vein. So we used the water we hauled for everything. Any warm or hot water was heated in big pans or from Mom's giant tea kettle on the big wood cook stove in the kitchen.

Out the kitchen window, there was a narrow yard between the side of the house and the fence above the garden. Next to the fence in a shady spot where the water ran into the garden on the side of the house, Mom had a patch of tansy. I don't know anyone else who grew tansy. It's a green fern that doesn't grow too tall. It has a pleasant smell and works great when you want to add greenery to a bouquet of flowers. When you cut the tansy off, it grows back.

≈

Once a week, usually Sunday night, we went to Grandma and Grandad's house for baths. It felt so good to get a bath in a real bathtub and have my long hair washed and rinsed with plenty of warm water. We didn't fill the bathtub more than a few inches and we didn't change water between baths. Grandma and Grandad had a good producing spring but four baths in a row would probably have taxed the water supply. Mom usually bathed last and she said the water was getting pretty cool and dirty by then. The flush toilet was nice too. The rest of the week we washed up with warm water using a washcloth and soap in a white enamel dishpan we called the wash basin. We called these wash-ups either a "spit bath" or "giving it a lick and a promise".

For our baths, Mom bought bath oils for us or we got them as gifts. They smelled so good, made your skin soft and were pretty to look at. Round bubbles of oil about ½ inch in diameter held oil in translucent red, green and yellow colors. Throwing two or three of those bath oils under the hot water tap in the tub, it was fun to watch the container dissolve and the colored oil disperse. One time, I got fancy bath powder in a pretty pink round plastic box as a gift. I loved the smell of the powder and the fluffy powder puff that was round and the same size as the powder box. But honestly, I didn't get the concept. When I put it on, it felt like my skin was dusty, but nice smelling.

When we had baths, it was a treat to spend the evening at Grandma and Grandad's house because we watched television (black and white). Ed Sullivan and Red Skeleton were favorites. Television reception came from an antenna on the roof of the house. Grandma and Grandad could receive two channels, both out of Grand Junction. One carried CBS programming and I think the other was NBC. After our baths, Mom made popcorn. Until someone gave us an air-popper one Christmas, it was popped in oil in a pan on the stove. Hot buttered, salted popcorn. Yum.

≈

Often, Mom used the phone to call Grandma Cole, her mother, in New Castle. Grandma and Grandad were on a party line. In their case, it was a two-party line. So if it rang once, it was for the Hall family down the road. If it rang twice, it was for Grandma and Grandad. Of course, it was bad phone etiquette and very rude, but one party could listen in on the other party's conversation. More commonly, you might pick up the phone to make a call and realize there was a phone call already in progress. Then it was a quick "oops, sorry" and you hung up the phone and tried again later. The system worked pretty well unless one · party was extremely talkative and spent all day or all night on the phone.

The most annoying thing was if a child was playing with the phone or the phone accidentally was left off the hook at the other party's house and you wanted to make a call. You could always yell into the phone and hope someone on the other end was close enough to hear you. That usually didn't work. So you'd either have to keep trying and wait until they noticed the phone and hung up, or actually drive to their place and knock on the door. That usually wouldn't work either because ranch folks are hardly ever in or near the house during the day.

≈

My grandparents had an electric/woodburning cook stove and wood/coal heating. We had electricity at our house but only for the lights and small appliances. Our heating and cooking was from coal and wood. The cook stove was huge and took up much of the kitchen. Made of cast iron, the stove top had four heavy round lids on the left and a flat surface on the right, over the oven. The lids were heavy and awkward even when the fire was out. When they were hot, there was a special tool to lift them. There was a small door in the front of the firebox where Mom set the fire with kindling and paper. After the fire was going, coal or wood was added through the lids on the top of the stove.

How hot or fast the fire burned in the cook stove depended on the fuel and the air intake. This was tricky but Mom was an expert at it. Coal was great for stoking the fire and keeping it going for hours at a time. Hard wood like spruce, pine, oak or fruit trees burned for a long time but wasn't extremely hot. If you wanted a quick, hot fire, like for cooking a meal in the summer, quakie was the best. Quakie or Aspen are the nicknames used by locals for the Quaking Aspen trees that were prevalent in the high country above about 7000 feet in elevation. Mom liked quakie in the summer when it was hot because she could cook a meal and then let the fire go out without heating up the house too much. In our living room was a big heating stove that burned both coal and wood.

Several small coal mines were operating in the area around where we lived. They sold lump coal by the ton and we hauled it home in our pickup. The small pieces were called nut coal. The coal was unloaded into a pile in the coal shed which was down the hill and across the creek from our house. Now they're considered antiques, but we had a couple of coal buckets and a coal shovel. Coal buckets had an elongated spout on one side of the rim so it was easier to pour chunks of coal from the bucket into the stove than it would have been from a regular bucket. The coal shovel was small and flat, useful for scooping up a few small chunks of coal out of the bucket and putting it into the stove or scooping the ashes out of the stove when you cleaned it.

Lump coal was nice for stoking the fire, especially at night, and making it last for long periods of time without going out. But sometimes the chunks were too big to fit into either of our stoves so Mom had a short handled sledge hammer in the coal shed that she used for breaking up the larger chunks of coal.

Mom and Dad cut firewood throughout the summer. Our firewood was spruce, pinon, cedar, oak brush and quakie. Sometimes people gave us the wood from fruit trees they cut down. Wood from fruit trees and cedar smelled really good when it was in the wood box or burning in the stove. Grandma and Grandad subscribed to the Grand Junction Daily Sentinel, the Rifle Telegram, and the Glenwood Post. So we always had plenty of newspaper to start fires. If there were any old boards around, Dad sawed them into lengths that would fit in the stove and Mom split them into kindling.

The stoves created a lot of ashes and had to be cleaned out often. In winter, Mom dumped some of the ashes where we parked the pickup to help with traction on the mud and ice. Even though we were careful and tried to pull all the old nails out of anything we burned, sometimes one would be missed and sure enough, the pickup tire would seek it out and go flat. Along with the ashes, there were often clinkers in the bottom of the stove. These were chunks of coal that were really mostly rock so they didn't burn. We used clinkers to make what Mom called "Depression Flowers." I thought it looked like a miniature magical crystal city, like the Emerald City in "The Wizard of Oz." The recipe came from Great Grandmother Rosa Arthur.

- One porous clinker or cinder.
- Mix and pour on top of clinker: 2 Tblspn liquid Bluing, 3 Tblspn salt, ½ cup water.
- Mix and pour on top: 3 Tblspn salt, 3 Tblspn bluing.
- 7 or 8 drops of mercurochrome dropped around on top for color.
- Will take 24 hours to grow.

We thought it was great fun, mixing and pouring, then watching the delicate crystals bloom and grow. In a couple of days, the flowers would dissolve but they were fun and very pretty while they lasted.

The living room had a fireplace but we didn't use it much because the stove was more efficient. The fireplace, and it's chimney on the outside of the house, was made of river rock, probably collected from nearby East Divide Creek. It was huge, taking up almost all of one wall of the living room. The fireplace had a mantle where Mom put family photos and knickknacks. It was a great place for hanging stockings at Christmas time.

The thought of crawling out of a nice warm bed on winter mornings made you want to stick your head under the quilt and play opossum. In the winter all of our beds had flannel sheets rather than regular cotton bedding. When Mom got the fire in the living room going each morning, she pulled two straight-backed chairs near the stove with the back of the chairs towards the stove. She laid our clothes on the backs of the chairs to warm, then got us out of bed. We were very quick about running across the cold linoleum floors straight to the stove where we each jumped up on the chairs to get dressed.

We girls weren't a lot of help with the coal, wood and water chores. I think Mom had so much to do each day that rather than nag us to help, it was just easier to go ahead and do it herself. But I must have watched her or helped enough to learn how to do things the best and most efficient way. For example, Mom could stand a piece of wood on the chopping block and chop, chop, chop, she had a pile of kindling in no time. I'm sure much of the time Mom thought her life revolved around chopping wood, taking ashes out and hauling coal, wood and water to the house, day in and day out. I don't know how many trips she made to the coal shed and back to the house every day to keep the coal buckets and the wood and kindling boxes full.

Carrying armloads of wood or kindling was an art. The goal is to carry as much as you can so you don't have to make as many trips from the woodshed to the house. Mom always carried the wood in one arm because she had a full coal bucket in the other hand. If you're right handed, your right arm is often the strongest. So crook that arm at the elbow to make a 90 degree angle. With your other hand, starting at the elbow, lay pieces of wood or kindling along your arm to your hand and stack the wood up from there. Weight and balance are key here. And don't be too ambitious. If you get your armload of wood so tall or so heavy you're going to drop all or some of it before you get to the house, you might as well make two trips. For little kids, or people that don't know how to carry wood, using both arms is best. But you need a partner to load you up.

In the winter, skunks liked to dig a hole and work their way in under our house. It was nice and warm under there because of the heat from our stoves so I know they had nice cozy nests and dens under the house. They also had their young there in the spring. Generally, we all coexisted in peace and everything was fine.

But when things went bad, it was really bad. Sometimes, and it happened at least once if not more often each winter, one of our cats and the skunks would get into a fight. When that happened, one hundred percent of the time the skunks won. They immediately scented off, sending the cat scrambling out from under the house. Besides the poor kitty's problems, the skunk odor then began to permeate through our house and settle into everything in it, especially our clothes.

When our dogs were directly sprayed by a skunk, we tried bathing them in tomato juice but I really don't think it helped much. With cats, don't even think about it. If the smelly cat was normally an indoor/outdoor kitty, we tried to make sure they stayed outside until the smell wore off. About the only remedy for skunk odor is time. Even though it was winter, Mom opened doors and windows to get a little fresh air moving through the house. All of that was annoying and inconvenient but we managed. The really hard thing for us was going to school. After being in the smelly house and wearing the clothes for a period of time, we tended to get somewhat used to the odor. But if we went outside and then back in the house, the odor seemed fresh and strong again.

Even worse was when we got on the school bus and into the classroom at school. We couldn't stay out of school because it took several days for the odor to weaken and go away from our clothes. Mom did her best but washing the clothes didn't help and neither did hanging them outside in the fresh air. So we went to school. Kids can be cruel. We were already mortified to be going to school smelling like skunk. The laughter and taunts of the other kids made us feel worse.

≈

Dad and Grandad both had big toolboxes with every tool they might need. I don't recall that we had any power tools, except maybe a drill. We also had trouble lights for use in dark places like underneath equipment or in engine compartments. Of course, that only worked if they were close enough to an electrical outlet to plug the light in which didn't happen very often. Machinery never breaks down at convenient times or places. We had flashlights everywhere. They were in glove compartments, under car and tractor seats, in tool boxes, kitchen drawers, under pillows and on nightstands. When it was dark at our place, it was very, very dark.

When Daddy was working on something, it seemed to me to always involve nuts and bolts. We girls helped though I imagine sometimes we were more of a hindrance than a help. Helping usually involved fetching tools and holding bolts, nuts and washers in our hand so they wouldn't get lost. We were very good at finding a flat or Phillips head screwdriver. We knew the difference between open ended and closed end wrenches. Some of the wrenches had an open end on one end of the wrench and a closed end on the other. So if Dad asked for a three-quarter or five-eighths wrench, we could get one and he could pick which end he needed to use. We also learned that sometimes he wasn't a very good guesser as to the size of the nut. So if Dad asked for a 7/8" wrench, we brought him that one but also wrenches just a little smaller and just a little bigger than that. It also helped us know fractions in a practical sense before we ever learned them at school.

When we weren't near a toolbox, there was usually a crescent wrench handy. It's amazing what Mom and Dad could accomplish with just a screw driver, a crescent wrench and a pair of pliers. The crescent wrench had a thumbscrew that moved the jaws of the wrench wider apart or closer together. The correct size of wrench was always better, of course, but the crescent wrench did the job too. Once in awhile, the corners on a nut got worn and rounded because someone had put it on too tight. Until Dad got the offending nut off and tossed it, there was usually a lot of cussing going on. When the threads on the screw itself got stripped, that was even worse. Then a replacement screw or bolt had to be found.

We had several coffee cans of old nails, nuts, bolts, washers and screws. I don't know where they all came from. I used to wonder if whatever piece of machinery or equipment they had originally come from was now running or working, missing a bolt, or several. Dad was always looking for a bolt or nut of a specific size for one thing or another.

Little metal boxes with plastic drawers were very popular at the time. We got Mom one for a birthday or Christmas present which she kept at the house. It had various sizes of washers, bolts, nuts and screws, washers and nails. It also had thumbtacks, butterfly nuts, fuses for Christmas lights and the car, hooks of various shapes and sizes and those neat little screws that expand in sheetrock and are great for hanging pictures on the wall. Almost any little gadget you needed you could find in Mom's organizer

Though we were told that if we took something (hammer, saw, screwdriver, whatever) to always, without fail, put things back where we found them. We tried to remember to do that but sometimes we forgot (so did Dad). So next time someone needed that hammer or screwdriver, it was a scavenger hunt to find it. So Mom gathered up a hammer, crescent wrench, flat and Phillips head screwdrivers, hack saw and a pair of pliers and kept them in a shoe box in the house. Those tools we all took more seriously because she meant it when she said make sure you bring those things back. She threatened to paint them all pink so Daddy would return them.

Where do you always find something you've lost or misplaced? You find it in the last place you look. Very funny. When we told Mom we couldn't find something, she always gave us good, helpful advice. She would ask first if we'd looked anywhere but the ceiling. Then she told us to remember the last time we saw whatever we were looking for, then backtrack from there to all the places we were from the time we last saw whatever we were looking for.

We had regular pliers, needle nose pliers and lots of different sizes and lengths of flat and Phillips head screwdrivers. Needle nose pliers let you hold things in hard to reach places. Regular pliers were handy for many things and usually someone was carrying a pair of pliers in the hip pocket of their jeans. I thought it was cool how you could hold something up to about an inch wide or you could cock the jaws and hold something quite a bit bigger. Or you could cut a piece of wire. Pliers were often used to twist a piece of baling wire to hold something securely in place, then to cut the ends of the wires shorter.

Mom had a tiny little set of tools for the sewing machine that was kept in the sewing machine drawer and nobody touched those. Sometimes she used those tiny little screwdrivers to tighten screws in hers or Grandma and Grandad's glasses.

For really big jobs, we had a heavy duty monkey wrench. We had all sorts of saws – regular saws, hacksaws, meat saws, double handled saw and, of course, the chain saw. We had claw hammers, ball-peen hammers and sledge hammers. And if we were someplace where no hammer was handy, my folks were good at improvising. We had a couple of hatchets that were handy for chopping kindling but my folks were known to turn the head of the hatchet around and use it as a hammer in a pinch. It's especially useful for pounding in tent stakes and stakes at the head and foot of the rows in the garden. We had a regular axe and a double headed axe. Dad kept the hatchets and axes sharp so chopping wood was easier. Trying to chop wood with a dull axe is an exercise in frustration. You might as well use a sledge hammer.

One of the most valuable tools on the ranch, in terms of getting heavy work done efficiently, was Dad's big welder. We were told how dangerous it was and warned to stay away. Dad had a metal welder's hood and heavy duty leather gloves and chaps to protect him from the sparks. We stayed far out of the range of the sparks and whenever he flipped the welder's hood down, we quickly either turned away or covered our eyes with our hands.

My dad didn't claim to be much of a mechanic and in fact, always made a bit of a show about how he didn't like fixing things. But it seems like he was always fixing or working on one thing or another. Mom said our idea of repairs was that anything could be fixed if you had plenty of "bubble gum and baling wire." Later that was amended to include duct tape and a can of WD40 as well.

Fixin' Fence 4

The driveway into Grandma and Grandad Arthur's place was about a mile and a half below ours.. A big mailbox marked the driveway that took a little dip down to a wooden gate. This is where the gravel ended. All of the lanes and roads on the ranch itself were dirt, either very dusty or very muddy. There was no in-between except maybe after a nice little rain that would cut the dust and dampen the ground. Many of the places we drove to on the ranch couldn't be called a road at all. We simply drove across the hayfield or pasture to wherever we were going.

The rule in the west is to leave a gate as you find it. If it's open, leave it open. If it's closed, you'd better make sure it's closed, and stays closed, after you go through it.

Unfair as I thought it was, it seemed to be another kids' job to open the gate, wait for the pickup or car to go through, close the gate then run to jump back in the pickup. Opening and closing a wooden gate like the one at

Grandma and Grandad's was no big deal because it swung open and closed on its hinges. Some wooden gates had a supporting fence post that may have sagged. Then the gate would need to be dragged through the dirt to get it wide enough for a pickup to go through.

The most important thing about closing a gate was to be very sure the chain or wire holding the gate closed was secure. This responsibility only had to be neglected once for the lesson to be learned. Chasing cows or horses that got out because you didn't get the gate closed was not only dusty and thirsty work but also humiliating. Even though the adults would never actually say anything about it, it was obvious they were none too pleased to be spending their afternoon rounding up animals that were where they were supposed to be until "someone" didn't get the gate shut.

The other type of gate on the ranch was made of barbed wire, just like the fences. The gate to the lane into our house was made from barbed wire. When we moved in, there was a wooden gate. It eventually fell apart so Mom and Dad built a barbed wire gate. Apparently Grandad didn't think they got it tight enough so shortly after they built the gate, he tightened it. The old wooden gate wasn't taken away but lay back against the clematis vines and bushes near the gateway. It became part of the landscape, much the same as those old root cellars and log cabins you see when driving along roads in the mountains.

A barbed wire gate was wired and stapled to the last post of the existing fence where you wanted to anchor the gate as if it were another span of fence. Fencing staples looked like a nail about two inches long that had been bent in the middle and was sharp on both ends.

The other end of the gate was the interesting part. A loop of baling wire was stapled near the top of the post where the gate would be secured and another loop near the bottom of the same post. To close this gate, you put the bottom of the post at the unsecured end of the gate in the lower loop of wire, then put the top of the post against your shoulder and push like mad, snagging the top loop over the top of the post the instant it would reach. Do the process in reverse to open the gate. The goal was to have the gate as tight as the fence on either side of it.

Barbed wire gates were the bane of my young existence. It felt like a rite of passage from girlhood to adulthood when I was actually able to open and shut a barbed wire gate. It seemed as a matter of case (or contrariness) that whoever built the gate purposely made it a few inches too short to span the space needed. The explanation was that the gate needed to be good and tight with no sagging. The practical result was that a person with a smaller physique (a girl, for example) really had to get her shoulder against the gate post and throw all of her weight into it to open or close a gate. Of course to us, failure and the disdain of the adults was not pleasant so we'd do our level best to open and shut that gate. Sometimes it was all we could do to get the tip of the post in the bottom loop and just barely get the loop over the top of the gate post. If it held, it was good enough for us.

Fixing fence was a never ending job. Weather and animals took their toll on the fences. Cows and horses like to carefully put their chest up against the fence and then lean into it. Apparently our cows were the ones that came up with the saying "the grass is always greener on the other side of the fence".

Once we found that the back fence of our upper pasture was actually cut by a snowmobiler so they could easily get to the Bureau of Land Management (BLM) public land behind our place. What was even more maddening to my folks was there was a barbed wire gate only a couple of spans away from where the fence was cut.

Barbed wire gates on the ranch weren't only where there were well defined or often used roads. Many gates allowed access from one pasture or field to another and we all learned where those gates were. If you were on foot, you could climb through the fence between the strands of barbed wire. But if you were driving, riding horseback or moving cows from one place to another, you needed a gate. There were also gates from our property to other people's property and to the public lands (BLM) around our place. These gates were found every quarter of a mile or so, whatever seemed conveniently located and made sense given the terrain and possible uses of the gate. Shared, or common fences implies shared maintenance but I don't remember anyone ever fixing fence around our place except us.

Our barbed wire fences were either three or four strands. A strand was one length of barbed wire. So on a four strand fence with a six foot fence post, figure out four evenly-spaced strands, starting with the lowest strand about a foot off the ground. Fence posts were buried in the ground every ten or twelve feet, maybe closer, depending upon the terrain.

If a tree was handy, it was used and you had one less post hole to dig, by hand, in the hard Rocky Mountain dirt. Maybe the fence wouldn't be straight from one post to the next but it was a lot easier to wrap, tighten and staple four strands of barbed wire to the tree than waste those scarce fence posts and dig the post hole. If a fence was several decades old, you can see where the tree has grown up around the barbed wire, making the fence and the tree part of the same thing. In between the fence posts were three or four equally spaced stays. Stays were smaller around than fence posts and not buried but simply wired to the fence strands with baling wire to help keep the wires evenly spaced.

Barbed wire was secured to fence posts with fencing staples. So someone was always carrying an old three pound coffee can with a wire handle that held the staples and a staple puller that doubled as a hammer and a wire cutter. The staple puller was like a pair of pliers with extra gadgets. No one went anywhere on the ranch without some sort of pliers or staple puller. It seems like there was always something wired together that had to be either tightened or cut. If you didn't have staples, you could use a nail, pound it in half way, bend it over and pound the head of the nail into the cedar post. Staples were great because you could secure the barbed wire to the fence post and then give it a couple more whacks to slightly depress the head of the staple into the wood. That barbed wire wasn't going to slip. Any used staples were put in the bucket, to be straightened later and reused.

A coil of baling wire was in the staple bucket or someone's pocket for attaching stays. Ranch families were very much into the reuse, recycle mode long before it became popular. When building fence, every so often a length of barbed wire was coiled and hung over a fence post so it would be handy for future repairs. Often fixing fence involved a lot of walking so the less to carry, the better.

Every spring, someone walked the fences. Besides finding where one or more strands of wire were snapped, or a post was rotted off, we would eyeball every post to see if staples needed to be replaced or re-seated into the post. If a fence post had broken or rotted off, it must be replaced. If you could cut a new post from any nearby cedars, that was just great. Otherwise, a post had to be found or, worst case, you'd have to go back to the house to get one out of a small stack of previously cut fence posts. Metal fence posts were available at the Co-op but that was an expense we didn't need and my family thought the wooden posts stayed upright better. I thought they looked nicer too. Once a new post was found and it was verified there was enough spare barbed wire to make the repairs, it was all man and shovel against hard rocky dirt. Good heavy leather work gloves were an absolute must as were long sleeves, no matter how hot the day was.

The post was generally eight feet tall and the post hole needed to be at least three feet deep. The posthole circumference was enough for the post and a couple of inches extra all the way around so the diameter of the hole was maybe eight or ten inches. It's easy to say "two feet deep and ten inches across" but not so easy to accomplish. Once the hole was dug with nice, neat, steep sides and all the loose dirt piled near the hole, the post was dropped into the hole and thumped against the bottom a few times.

Now a small amount of dirt was shoveled into the hole, all around the post. This is the same dirt that had just been shoveled out of the hole. Before too much dirt was in the hole, one of we kids would hold the post up straight, or what we thought was straight. Dad would step away and look at the post from all directions, directing us to tilt the post an inch this way, a smidge that way until he was satisfied it was straight. Then, he turned the shovel over and the end of the handle was used to tamp, tamp, tamp the dirt. Repeat shoveling and tamping until the hole has been filled in, level with the ground. The more packed the dirt was around the post, the longer it would stand straight.

The post was in and it was time to get a drink of water from the jug and sit in the shade of a nearby tree for a minute. Our water jug was always an old Clorox bottle that Mom washed thoroughly. Then she filled it halfway full of water and put it in the freezer. When we needed a water jug, we'd take one out of the freezer and fill the jug on up to the top with water. The ice melted over the course of the day and we had nice cold water even on the hottest days. The water jug was sometimes the most important tool when doing ranch work. A big drink of cold, clear water is a great reward for a job well done.

Besides helping carry the staple bucket, staple puller, shovel, extra wire and water jug, kids often carried a heavy and awkward tool called "the stretcher". This contraption (ours was yellow) was made of heavy cast iron with lots of moving parts. It was very useful and very dangerous, a fact of which my Dad reminded us every time we were fixing fence. I've never seen it but my Dad's horror story was if the wire was stretched too tight and snapped, it could whip around and take your head off. It was essential to keep the strands of barbed wire as tight as possible when either building or fixing fence and the stretcher gave you extra leverage to make that happen. If the fence posts are solid in the ground and the barbed wire is stretched tight, the whole fence is going to last longer without sagging wire and leaning posts.

Since this was a new fence post, using the stretcher was not quite as tricky as repairing fence in the middle of a span, but still as dangerous. A loop about three inches wide was fashioned on the end of the strand of wire still attached to the fence. One end of the length of spare wire to be used for the repair was put through that loop and bent to make its own loop. Each loop was twisted good and tight with pliers. One end of the stretcher was snagged securely around the new post. The other end of the spare wire was inserted into the other end of the stretcher and locked into the tool. A handle on the stretcher activated a come-along system that pulled the wire tight. It must be very tight but not so stressed the wire breaks. The end of the wire was wrapped around the new post and securely stapled in place. The tension on the stretcher was released and that repair was complete.

When repairing a break in the middle of the fence, each end of the wire was inserted into each end of the stretcher and locked into place. The wires were stretched as tight as possible and as was safe, and looped together. The stretcher was released and we moved on down the fence line. Our family was very good at fence building so usually there weren't too many repairs to be made in the miles and miles of fence on the ranch. An unspoken on any ranch with no surplus of workers is that it's always better to do anything right the first time, even if it takes some time, than to have to go back and do it again.

Pickup Trucks and Tractors   5

We had various adventures and misadventures with our vehicles.

One time the car was parked across the bridge from the house. When we went out in the morning, a huge limb from an equally huge cottonwood tree had fallen on our car. It mostly hit the trunk of the car so the front of the car was okay. The back window and backseat side windows were completely smashed and there were small bits of shiny glass inside the car and all around on the ground. The car was a 1950s era Ford. It was blue and white. I don't know how we got around while the car was being fixed, or even if we got it fixed at all. I remember all the bits of glass sparkling in the sun like jewels.

After the car, we got a Scout, also blue in color. It was great for narrow rutted roads because it was short and had good clearance. It wasn't very big but it was big enough to carry the four of us and all of our stuff. The most distinctive thing about the Scout was it seemed to always be breaking down. Dad was never much of a mechanic nor did he claim to be. But necessity is the mother of invention so for someone who didn't much like the work, Dad spent a fair amount of time fixing things that had broken down.

One time something serious happened with the Scout and Daddy had to take it all apart. I got an old rug or something like Dad had and climbed under the Scout, laying on my back on the ground like he was, and pretending to work on the car too. Mom loves to tell the story that when he finally got it back together, he had a coffee can of "leftover" parts. Even more astounding was the Scout actually ran.

Grandma and Grandad drove a black Ford Galaxy with red interior. They kept the inside immaculate. We didn't ride with them very often. They kept that car for many years. After the Galaxy, they had a big white Ford LTD. Grandma never drove. She drove a tractor once in awhile when we needed her. Grandma and Grandad had to be at home every morning and evening to milk the cows. But on summer afternoons, they often got in the car and went for a drive. I don't think they had a specific destination or route in mind, just wanted to get out and enjoy the day driving around on county roads past nearby ranches and farms and up in the high country.

There was a 1948 GMC pickup parked in the driveway by Grandma and Grandad's house. It was parked in a back corner, past the big gas tank on its metal stand and they called it "the Jimmy." The hood, which had been red, was rusted almost all the way through, springs popped through the upholstery of the bench seat and we kids spent many happy times "driving" the pickup and playing pretend. At some point, the pickup got painted a bright barn red and they got it running. It looked pretty sharp. We didn't use it on the ranch but we did use it one summer when Mom drove to Delta to pick up mink feed.

We had some big boat of a car when I was in junior high and early high school. It might have been a Buick. We thought it was funny because it was such a big car and though it had a standard transmission, you shifted gears on the steering column. We liked the car because it had an 8-track tape player and whoever had the car before us left several tapes we could play. We were all very proud of that old (new to us) car because it was the first time we were a two-car family.

The car was big enough to haul us and our friends to school sports and other events. Mom was always ready and happy to do it and I don't remember riding with other moms, especially long distance. Sometimes, Aunt Ruthie Whitman went with us. It seems we were often on slick roads or in a snowstorm, usually late at night on the way home from a football or basketball game in Meeker, Craig or Steamboat Springs. It never seemed to bother Mom but maybe she put on a good front for our benefit. Aunt Ruthie says "Bet did the driving and I provided the courage." Mom never made us feel like it was a chore to drive us around and I know our friends felt the same way. Lots of times friends said, "Your Mom is so nice!" That was true. She was very nice, available when we needed her and dependable too. Anyway, we could pack a lot of kids in that big car.

None of our cars or pickups had air conditioning, electric windows or cruise control. Most of them were not automatic transmission and didn't have power steering. We usually had an AM/FM radio but that was the extent of your listening enjoyment and depended entirely on whether the reception was any good or not. At the best of times we only got two or three AM stations because we only had two or three stations in nearby towns. To aid with reception, cars with radios had an antenna, or what we called an aerial. The aerial was a thin round piece of metal tubing that stood about three feet tall. It was on the right side of the car to the right of the hood and directly in front of the passenger side windshield. The aerial was flexible to a certain extent so if it was bumped by a tree branch or something, it would give way and spring back. Still, it was common to break aerials off when driving through brush, trees or a bunch of cows, especially in some of the tight spaces Dad got us into in the high country.

This was when drivers actually had to drive. The driver supplied the power for steering and shifted gears by watching the tachometer, if there was one, or simply by listening to the engine or by feel. If you've ever driven a pickup or big car without power steering, you'll know sometimes it took some serious arm power to turn the wheel and steer the vehicle. Steering wheels were bigger then too. Probably so the driver could get a good grip to wrench the wheel around. And be careful how you curve those thumbs around the wheel because if you hit a bump or rut in the wrong way, the steering wheel might be jerked away from you and turn hard one direction or the other with no notice, almost taking your thumbs off at the same time. My Mom often said, "give 'em forty acres and they'll turn that thing around." I think she was referring to hard-to-turn steering wheels but mostly she was commenting about some driver that couldn't manage to turn a vehicle around without lots of space and lots of time.

When some people started getting air conditioning in their new cars, my folks teased that we had air conditioning too. It depended on how many windows there were and how fast you were going. For instance, 4/60 air conditioning meant you had four windows rolled down and were going 60 miles an hour. Driver and passenger windows were literally rolled down and up manually using a crank handle on the inside the door. The driver and front seat passenger windows also had a small, elongated-triangle-shaped window in the front of the regular window called a wing. When the wing was unlatched, it tilted in and out so air was directed into the car when you were moving. It could be adjusted so you got a little air or a lot. Using the wing, you got cool air into the car without rolling down the big window and either freezing or blowing everybody else out of the car.

Except for those cars, an old jeep, and the Scout, my parents usually owned and drove what we called a pickup. Others might call it a pickup truck or simply a truck. The pickup we had for many years was a 1968 blue Ford ¾ ton, four wheel drive outfit, heavy duty and with a long bed and a propensity for breaking u-joints. Can you tell that blue was Daddy's favorite color? Mom's was red but she got overridden when it came to our vehicles. We were all very familiar with the sound of a u-joint about to go out and Daddy kept a spare behind the bench seat in the cab of the pickup. The pickup had two gas tanks which was great because we could go to the high country for a day or a week without having to worry about running out of gas or hauling gas cans along. You filled up the tanks just behind the door on each side of the pickup. There was a switch on the dashboard that let you switch from using one tank to using the other.

Besides being our every day family car, we used our pickup for hauling loads of whatever needed to be hauled. It was also good for getting through mud holes without getting stuck, for making headway through several inches of snow on unplowed roads, and for giving a lift to baby calves that just couldn't make the trip from the ranch to the upper pasture. No task was too big or too small.

Tire chains, a logging chain for towing, an axe and a shovel were kept in the back of the pickup year round just in case. There were lots of times Mom or Dad pulled out the logging chain to pull someone out of the ditch or tow a car or pickup that wouldn't start. These chains were heavy duty with big cast iron hooks on each end.

We also had a handy man jack in the pickup. It was much more versatile and heavy duty than the tire jack that came with the pickup. The handy man could be used for changing tires, of course. Also it might be used for leverage when stuck in a mud hole and you didn't have a winch. This was a messy business because you had to get down in the mud hole and stand the jack up by burying it in the mud as close to the stuck tire as possible. Then jack it up as far as you can without tipping the jack over in the mud. Get in the pickup, drive off the jack and hope all four tires dig in and you're un-stuck. If the stuck tire is still spinning, set up the jack and repeat. In my experience, my folks always managed to get out. Eventually.

We only put the pickup in four wheel drive when we needed it. On steep or rocky terrain, you shifted down. To go into four wheel drive was a two step process. The first step, putting in the hubs, was mechanical and manual. That turned out to be another kid's job. I spent many wet, cold, muddy minutes jumping out of the pickup, setting the hub on the right front, then the left front. I don't think it mattered which tire you did first. I was familiar (intimately) with two types of mechanisms for putting in and taking out the hubs. I don't know if it was a style or design preference or if technology just changed.

On the Scout, the hub on each front tire was two parallel metal bars which you popped, swiveled and popped back into place. You did the same with the other bar then repeated the process on the hub on the other front wheel. On a newer pickup we had, there was a circular gadget you turned with your thumb and finger. You rotated it until you heard a small click and felt the hub lock in. If the hubs were hard to lock in or take out, the driver rolled the vehicle forward or backward a few inches until the hub easily locked into place. To engage the four wheel drive, there was a short gearshift next to the regular gear shift.

To increase the height of the pickup bed to haul big loads or animals, we had store-bought stock racks. They were a good investment and proved invaluable for things we needed to do around the ranch. The racks had short legs that fit into holes on the sides of the pickup bed. The racks extended up to about a foot over the top of the pickup cab and had a hinged gate that opened above the tailgate.

We put the racks on for hauling hay, firewood, bags of feed, camping gear; anything higher than the bed of the pickup. We also used it to move horses. One horse fit nicely in the back of the pickup. Loading the horse could be an adventure. Some horses were easy loaders. Some weren't. To load the horse, the pickup was backed up to a mound of dirt the height of the tailgate. Sometimes that would simply be backing the pickup so the rear wheels were in a ditch like at the side of the road. Sometimes there would be a mound of dirt someone had pushed up for this purpose.

After putting the tailgate down, someone held open the gate to the stock racks. Someone else led the horse straight towards the tailgate, stopping before going into the pickup and the horse would jump right in. That was the easy loader. As you might expect, this was not the norm and sometimes it took time and much cursing to get a horse loaded. If it couldn't be avoided, the person leading the horse could go on in the pickup, lead the horse in, and climb out over the stock racks. As with most things, the younger you started working with a colt to load, the easier it would be on both of you as the colt grew up.

Some horses might load easily but be nervous riders so we usually didn't haul them. Red Wing was a sorrel quarter horse, an old cow horse that had been on the ranch her whole life. She loaded fine but riding worried her so much she'd be in a cold sweat by the time you got wherever you were going. It was a bit of a thrill when the pickup started rocking back and forth as we were going down the road because Red wouldn't keep her feet still. But her favorite trick was to lean over the stock rack and blow snot in Daddy's ear through the open driver's side window. If possible, we hauled only well broke, gentle natured horses in the pickup. Generally, if we needed to move a horse, we rode it wherever we were going.

Grandad Cole had built a one horse trailer and when he didn't need it any more, he gave it to my parents. For some reason, we didn't use it much. As I recall, the tires were too small to handle rough and rutted roads, and it didn't pull very well at speeds over 30 or 40 miles per hour. Grandad had built it to pull behind his pickup in a much simpler, slower time.

In my experience with other people's horse trailers, you could still have all the same problems loading a horse as you did loading in the pickup. The horse didn't have to manage walking across the tailgate but they had to take a step up to get into the trailer. Either way some horses loaded like a dream and others were a nightmare. The best thing to do is to walk the horse around for a bit, then turn her towards the trailer or pickup without stopping. If the horse balks, try it again. When patience wore thin and time ran out, I've seen it where it took two or three men to load one horse. One person would lead the horse and the other two stood on either side of the horse, held a lariat tight against the horses' rump and pulled. There was usually a lot of sweet talking the horse which of course didn't help any more than cursing did.

The stock racks on our pickup were a favorite for the kids. In good weather, we rode in the back of the pickup and when the stock racks were on, we'd climb as high up as we could while still holding on. On a warm summer day, the wind in our faces was cooling and exhilarating. If the stock racks weren't on, we had to sit on the bed of the pickup, or at the most on the wheel wells. That wasn't as much fun.

When we were on paved highways, going to town, we all rode in the cab of the pickup. This was long before seatbelt laws. Our newer pickups did have lap belts but only for the driver and one passenger and we didn't wear them. At the time, there was no such thing as car seats for children. Mom says the kid stood next to her while she was driving. She tucked us behind her shoulder and if something abrupt happened, she threw her right arm across to hold us from falling.

≈

Generally we moved hay from the field to the haystack or from the haystack to the field to feed the cattle in winter using a flat bed wagon. The wagon was on big sturdy wheels and pulled by a slow but reliable tractor. We had two tractors and in our usual descriptive way of naming things, we called them the big tractor and the little tractor. They were both red but I can't remember the makes. I think one of them was an International Harvester.

Neither of our tractors were very big, especially compared to what we see today. But they were big enough to get the job done on our ranch. The tractors didn't have cabs with air conditioning or shade. There was no radio. The tractor driver was out there in the elements. In the winter, if it was snowing or if it was clear and cold, sitting on the tractor chilled you clear through to the bone. On hot days the engine heat magnified and intensified the heat from the sun. Hay dust, gnats and grease from the tractor mixed with sweat soaked right through your shirt and into your skin.

The ranch had a 2 ton stock truck we didn't use often but it worked well for jobs too big for the pickup. I don't remember much about it except Dad first got it when he and Uncle Ernie did some logging in the high country. One time we hauled a bunch of calves to or from the sale. Another time, Grandad fell out of the back of the truck and broke his collar bone. At some time when I was a kid it got painted. The cab was blue. The stock racks were hinged and folded up or down against the outside of the truck as needed. The racks were painted red and the parts that folded down were white so our truck was red, white and blue.

Buying the swather (or windrower) was a big deal on the ranch. It was an Owatana and mostly yellow and orange. It was very expensive but it saved time and work during haying season. The swather would cut the hay and put it in windrows for baling at the same time. Before the swather, the hay was mowed with a tractor and mower. Then it was raked into windrows with a tractor and rake so it could be baled. This meant handling the mowed hay twice, taking twice the time and work for Dad and Grandad. Also, more of the leaves from the alfalfa dropped off, making the hay less nutritious for the cattle and horses. Swathing or mowing the hay was strictly Dad's job. The baler was pulled by a tractor and no one but Grandad ran the baler.

Other equipment was used on the ranch, all pulled by a tractor. When hayfields needed to be re-seeded with alfalfa, we had a plow to turn the dirt. There was a disc to break up the clods, a harrow for spreading the dirt, clods and manure evenly across the field, and a planter to sow the alfalfa seed. There was the mower to mow the hay and the rake to pull the hay into windrows or turn it if it got rained on. We also had a manure spreader and a very old road grader for roads on the ranch. We didn't have the fancy equipment other places had but we had what we needed to get the job done with a minimum amount of upkeep and we didn't owe the bank anything for our equipment (except the swather).

If any of our equipment broke down, either Dad or Grandad worked on it, usually out in the field where it broke down. They carried a few tools in the tractors. If it was more serious, they'd drive it or tow it to the barn at Grandad's place or to our house, whichever was closer to where they broke down. Usually it wasn't anything wrong with the tractor but rather with the mechanism that made the baler bale, the swather mow, etc.

Grandad kept a 500 gallon gas tank on a tall metal stand across the driveway from their house. It was only for ranch use, though I think Grandma and Grandad filled up their car with it. Mom always filled up our pickup in town. When the big gas tank needed gas, Grandad called the Co-op in Silt who came to fill it.

≈

Helping someone tow a car or pickup seemed like a very scary business and when I grew up and had to help, I found out I was right. It wasn't dangerous if everyone was careful, which we always were. The scary part was actually coordinating the tow between two people and not messing it up so the chain broke about the same time as the other person's temper. I had lots of practice watching Dad doing the towing and Mom in the other vehicle as the towee.

The shorter you can snug up the chain between the two vehicles, the better. A longer span gives more chances to break the chain. Mom or Dad backed the pickup as close to the other vehicle as possible. Then they had to climb under each vehicle to find something solid and sturdy to pull the chain around, then the hook was firmly hooked over the chain. If you hooked the hook itself to some part of the vehicle, it would probably slip off. If you attached the chain to the bumper, which would be the easiest thing to do, you might pull the bumper off. Once the chain is attached to both vehicles, there's some slack in the chain. Now comes the tricky part.

There are many reasons to tow a vehicle but the two most common in our lives were either the vehicle wouldn't start, or it was stuck in a mud hole or ditch. If it wouldn't start, usually you jumped it by connecting jumper cables between the battery of a running auto and the battery of the other. If you didn't have jumper cables, you could tow the vehicle. When the tow began, the towed vehicle would have the ignition turned on and the transmission in the lowest gear. Keeping the clutch pushed all the way to the floor, once you were moving a few miles per hour, the driver of the towed vehicle would pop the clutch and hope the engine kicked in.

If the engine did start, then you had to signal (holler, wave, honk) the person towing you at the same time as maintaining the same speed as the vehicle in front so you didn't break the chain. When they did stop, you had to keep from running into their rear bumper. Lots of chances to mess things up.

If the engine ran but you were stuck in a ditch or a mud hole, the tricky part was to engage the transmission at just the right moment when the towing vehicle has started moving and there is no slack in the chain but it's not too taut. Then, in theory, your vehicle helps the tow by easing on up out of the ditch at the same time you're being pulled out. If you start too fast or too jerky when trying to take the slack out of the chain, you can snap the chain quicker than a whistle and they're harder to fix than Dad's bad mood about the whole thing.

When I was a kid, none of our vehicles had a winch. I got the impression winches were another one of those things owned by people who had more money than we did. And besides, with my dad's "can do" attitude, who needs a winch anyway? Pickups and jeeps with winches had these huge contraptions attached to the front of the vehicle and had a motor that rolled the cable out and in. Dad pointed out that when you were stuck in a mud hole, how often were you close enough to a big rock or a big tree to which you could attach the winch anyway? Good point. Using the handy man jack, a shovel and a tow chain if another vehicle was with you were still the best ways to get a vehicle out of a mud hole or a ditch.

We always carried tire chains in the bed of the pickup just in case and I saw my parents put those chains on many times. This was especially true for Mom during hunting season when she sometimes had to make trips between hunting camp and town or the ranch. She was an expert and very efficient about putting tire chains on and taking them off. Most cars that weren't four wheel drive had rear wheel drive, so the use of tire chains was common.

Using tire chains might seem a daunting task but as with most things, a few simple facts and bits of knowledge simplified the process considerably. As with everything on the ranch, take care of those chains. Mostly that meant to never run them on dry, packed dirt or paved roads. When you hit pavement where snowplows had been through, take the chains off. Running them on pavement could break links in the chain that then had to be repaired. Putting on tire chains is not complicated but it takes some practice to get it right with a minimum of frustration. The secret is to get them tight enough to act like they are actually part of the tire. Once Mom got the chains too loose and they fell off and cut the brake line. Oops.

By the time you figure out that you need chains, you're either stuck or just can't make any forward progress. Once you pull over to the side of the road, trying to find a relatively flat spot, the fun begins. First, empty all the groceries, toys and other stuff from the bed of the pickup. Remove the spare tire and add it to the pile on the ground. Dig out the two tire chains. Put everything back in the bed. By now you can't feel your fingers or toes even though you're wearing heavy gloves and boots. Also, it's starting to get dark and there isn't a vehicle to be seen in either direction.

Dig as much snow out from around the rear tires as possible. Straighten out the chain and lay it on the ground in front of the tire. Get in and pull it forward so the tire is resting, hopefully fairly centered, on the chain. Pull the rest of the chain up and over the tire. Fasten the hook securely on both sides in the tightest link that will fit. This is the hardest part because you have to reach way under to get it hooked on the inside. Hook the rubber chain tightener in four links of the chain around the outside of the tire. Once chains are on both rear wheels, you should be good to go.

Boots, Hats and the Sale   6

I grew up as a thoroughly modern girl. Of course, modern in the context of the 1960s and 70s. Sure, everyone I knew except us had a TV and indoor plumbing, bathroom and running water. Mom cooked and heated the house with wood and coal. But all that was because we lived on the ranch, way out of a town. Being modern was how we thought and felt, not an inventory of the things we had or didn't have.

Every year, before the County Fair in the fall, Tammi and I each got a new pair of cowboy boots. Since we would wear them for a whole year if our feet didn't grow too much, picking out boots was important. We spent a lot of time getting the perfect color, height, toe shape, design and heel shape. There were several brands, but if they were on sale, we usually got Tony Lama. Dad said they were better boots but I think it was because Tony Lama and Dad rode the rodeo circuit at the same time and had met.

Boots were made of good sturdy leather and generally came to about halfway between ankle and knee. The leather was stiff and could rub sores on your shins, calves and feet if you didn't break them in properly. The style was for a pointed toe which we hated as we grew older and would seek out more rounded toes. The heels were square and about an inch tall. None of those beautiful tapered two or three inch heels we thought looked so cool. We would spend a lot of long days over the next year wearing the boots both walking and horseback so they needed to be just right.

When walking or running in leather boots, you don't want a high heel. The reason for a heel of any height was to help get the foot seated correctly in the stirrup and keep it from going on through the stirrup, effectively hanging the rider. If that happened and the rider got thrown, they would be drug rather than the boot coming out of the stirrup or the foot coming out of the boot. In the movies, that's a comical scene in every western. Not funny in real life. If your boot and foot got hung up in the stirrup, you would surely get kicked, drug, stepped on or much worse. If your boot came out of the stirrup like it was supposed to, you found yourself on the seat of your pants on the ground watching your horse kick up dust and head for the house. Then, the only thing that got hurt was your pride.

Dad and Grandad had both work boots and good boots but we kids only had the one pair. All of the boots had to be polished and shined often to protect the leather and make them look good. Surprise, this apparently was a kids chore. Sometimes, before polishing and buffing the shine, we used saddle soap to keep the leather pliant and avoid cracking. Applying saddle soap involved lots of tiring rubbing so it helped that I could do such chores with both my left and right hands and I would alternate.

Boot polish came in a flat can in various colors. We usually had black, brown and dark brown. One of those colors would do for most any color of boots we might buy. A can of boot polish was expensive but it lasted a long time and we used every last bit of it. The polish was applied by rubbing a clean rag against the polish in the can, then rubbing the polish on all parts of the boot except the sole. Once the polish was applied and rubbed in, we waited a few minutes for any moisture to evaporate. Then, taking another soft, clean rag we buffed the leather until there was a shine to be proud of. If you spent enough time and effort at it, you could make even old and bad looking boots look good. Sometimes, we wore our boots so much we wore the leather thin or even put a hole in the sole of the boot. Then we took them to town to Art's Shoes where the boot would be re-soled.

When you buy new boots, they fit when they feel as if they're way too small. It takes work to get that boot on your foot. If the boot slides on easily in the store, the leather will stretch and within a couple of weeks the boots will be too big and all the extra room will rub sores on your shins, heels and toes. Shove your toe and foot into the boot as far as they would go, then pull on the upper part of the boot until you finally got a soft pop and the boot slid onto your foot. When your boots are new, that's not as easy as it sounds. Luckily, boots have a sturdy leather tab on each side of the boot that you can stick your fingers through and pull like heck. With leverage and a little gritting of the teeth, the boot will eventually pop on.

It took a boot jack or a willing relative or friend to get the boots off. The best way was to sit on a chair or stool, have your helper stand with their backside to you and your booted foot between their legs. They held onto your boot with both hands. You put your free foot on your helper's behind and pushed. If done correctly, voila, you have a stocking foot and your helper has your boot. It sounds awkward, funny and slightly embarrassing but it really is the best way to get your boot off.

The boot jack was a poor second in my opinion. Usually made of wood, the main part of the gadget looked like a large, thick slingshot. It rested on a piece of wood about two inches tall and perpendicular to the other piece of wood. Standing up, you jammed the heel of your boot as far into the crack of the boot jack as possible. Then standing with your other foot on the back of the jack, pull with all your might and if it works, you have a stocking foot and the boot is still wedged in the bootjack.

New boots had to be broken in and there was no time saving or cutting corners with this task. I learned my lesson when I wore a pair of new boots for a few days without breaking them in properly and never skimped on that job again. The day after buying new boots, we started breaking them in. Just as with buying boots that didn't fit, if they weren't broken in properly, they would rub blisters on your heels, ankles and shins over the course of the year. The concept was to get those boots to precisely fit the shape of your particular feet. I imagine there were other ways to break in boots but on our ranch, there was only one way.

Simple in concept and profound in results, we put our brand new leather boots on and walked around in the creek until the leather was soaking wet. That's the easy and fun part. Now comes the hard part, you had to wear those boots nonstop until the leather was completely and totally dry. Uncomfortable for a day and half the night but for the rest of the year, you'd be glad you went through the ordeal.

We got new straw cowboy hats every year but one year, my parents decided we were old enough to take care of felt hats. Broadly speaking, felt hats were worn in the winter and straw hats were for summer. But on the ranch, for we kids anyway, straw hats were for every day and felt hats were for special things and going to town. We got our first felt hats when we were old enough to be in 4H and were going to show our horses at the County Fair so I was probably nine or ten years old. Felt cowboy hats were more expensive than straw and would last us for several years so picking out the right one was important. Dad and Grandad had both work hats and good hats. We would only have the one so we had to take care of it. When the hat looked dusty, we brushed it. I loved the dark brown or black hats best but soon found why Daddy and Grandad had at least one of their hats that was gray. The gray color didn't show the dust and dirt like the darker colors did.

When we were on the ranch, Grandad never went without his hat. I don't know how old his work hat was but it seemed ancient to me. Over the years, the brim had been bent and worked around so much it was just the way he wanted it. The sweatband was so dirty there was a good inch going around the hat that was darker gray than the rest of the hat from years of sweat, grease and dirt.

Grandma kept trying to get him to get a new hat but he wouldn't. He liked that one. He did have a good hat to wear to town.

All hats were removed indoors. It was impolite, disrespectful and quite simply, bad manners, to wear your hat in the house or in a restaurant or other public space indoors. It just wasn't done. Cowboy hats were never put on a chair or table with the brim down. You always put the hat on its top to avoid having the brim of the hat flattened. When buying a new hat, the shop keeper asked how you like the brim in terms of the curl on each side and shape of the front and back. He had a machine that steamed the hat and made it more pliable for shaping. After getting the hat home, each hat wearer made sure the shape was how they wanted it by curling the brim up or down until it held its shape. At home, there were wooden pegs on the wall or a set of mounted deer or elk antlers to hang your hat on. At someone else's house, you hung your hat on the back of your chair, or put it somewhere safe upside down. Nobody messed with your hat or even touched it. Those uninitiated to the finer art of hat etiquette were soon corrected. I don't remember Dad or Grandad ever wearing a baseball cap or going hatless much. They always wore their cowboy hats.

We got our new cowboy boots and jeans (always Levi's or Wranglers) at Wilson's Toggery in Rifle. It had a heavy wooden door with a bell that jangled whenever the door was opened. The store was fairly narrow and deep with a narrow aisle down the middle. On the left was a display counter with shelves of cowboy hats behind it and a steamer for shaping your hat. On the right were shelves and shelves of jeans. The rear of the store had lots of shelves of different brands, colors and sizes of boots and shoes. There were a couple of padded benches where you sat to try on boots or shoes near a tiny dressing room for trying on clothes. The clerk measured your foot with a handy little gadget. Then, after you chose the style and color of boots you liked, they disappeared through a door in the back and brought out boxes of boots for you to try on.

Every fall we got a new pair of school shoes and every summer, new sandals for going to town and a new pair of Keds. Keds were a brand of reasonably priced (cheap) tennis shoes. There were only a few brands and styles of what we called tennis shoes. The more expensive brands were sold at clothing stores like Penney's in Glenwood or Henry's in Rifle. Keds were bought at either of the two five & dime drugstores in Rifle – Ben Rex or the Corner Drugstore. Keds came in a few colors but I think ours were usually off-white. They were low cut on the ankle, made of canvas with rubber soles and flat laces. Keds were cool in summer, offered some protection from stickers, rusty nails and cactus and were easily washed. So we didn't have to take our shoes off for things like wading in the creek and tromping through mud puddles.

Living in the mountains, even on hot summer days, it was pretty cool in the evening. So we always had a sweatshirt with us. Most of them slipped over our heads. But we sometimes had the more expensive ones with hoods and pockets and zippers up the front. We saw other kids with Levi jackets and we always wanted our own. The thought was since we'd outgrow our clothes and only wear them one year, we got the less expensive sweatshirts and sweaters. We finally got our own Levi jackets when we were older and not growing so fast. Daddy had a denim jacket he wore all the time, year after year. He also had a lined one for when it got colder but not cold enough for a winter coat.

At home, we wore bobby socks, thin cotton socks that came up a couple of inches above the ankle. You folded the sock over neatly and evenly so the double layer of cotton protected your ankle from rubbing against your shoe. Unfortunately, bobby socks attracted every kind of weed, burr or sticker imaginable. On the ranch, everywhere you went you were walking through something that stuck to your socks, your jeans, or both. Cheat grass, cockle burrs, stick tights and other stickers attached themselves to our clothes, eventually working through the material enough to irritate your skin. There was no brushing the stickers off, you had to take the time to sit down and pull each sticker off, one by one.

≈

Sometimes on Saturday, we went to the sale. There was a livestock auction house (sale barn) in north Rifle and another in West Glenwood and they had a livestock sale very Saturday. They also had special sales as needed when they had a big consignment from one seller or there were a lot of people wanting to sell horses. Sometimes we would have some pigs, Holstein calves or young horses to sell, or we wanted to buy some livestock. But usually we just went for the excitement. The auctioneer, the bidders, the teenagers moving the animals in and out from the stock yards through the gates at each end of the ring was pure entertainment. Local farmers and ranchers dressed in their best going-to-town clothes and visited with each other. Going to the sale was a social event. Out of town buyers went from auction to auction to buy and sell livestock. They were easy to pick out in the crowd, mostly because of attitude and cigar smoke.

In front of the sale barn was a large parking lot to accommodate big trucks and trailers for hauling livestock. All around the sale barn outside were stockyards. There were loading chutes for the trucks and a series of small pens with lanes in between for the workers and animals to move through. At least some of the pens were lengths of wooden fence panels that could be moved as needed to change the size or configuration of lanes and pens. It all looked very complicated to me but the men running the stockyards knew what they were doing and things usually went smoothly.

Inside the door of the sale barn, to the left, was the café where they served burgers, fries, pie and coffee. There was the office where several clerks were busy handling transactions. The office had big glass windows so you could see all the activity going on. Spectators sat on wooden bleachers that formed a semicircle around the ring. In the center of the bleachers a couple of rows above the ring were 2 or 3 rows of several fold down, padded chairs instead of bleachers. This is where the buyers sat. Preferential treatment no doubt, but everyone honored it.

Across the sales ring was an elevated wooden platform where the auctioneer and clerk stood. The auctioneer at the Rifle Sale was J Gentry. They were always nicely dressed, the auctioneer in a yoked white western shirt and string tie or bolo tie and fancy felt hat; the secretary in a dressy western blouse, usually with lots of turquoise and silver jewelry. There was a loudspeaker system so the auctioneer had a microphone.

The sales ring was a small corral with a gate on each end and the livestock was brought into the building from the stock pens, through the gate. Once they were sold, the livestock was taken out through the other gate. The ring was made of pipe fencing and was not very big. If 10 or 15 cows were in the ring at any one time, it was pretty crowded. The floor of the ring was covered with fresh sawdust. The sale barn was pungent but not unpleasant. The mixture of sawdust, manure, dust, cigarette and cigar smoke and cooking smells from the kitchen permeated the place.

The ringmen working the livestock usually carried wooden canes. It seemed to me like the cane was more of an affectation, a badge of honor, than an actual tool. Once in awhile someone used their cane to poke an animal in the belly if they started going the wrong direction or strayed. After the livestock was brought in by the gatemen, the ringmen kept the animals moving in the ring so the buyers could see all sides of the animal, check their conformation and movement.

The auctioneer started the bidding at some predetermined amount based on the market at the time for the size, weight and age of the livestock being sold. There was a scale near the ring so everyone involved, seller, buyer, auctioneer, knew the weight of the livestock being sold. Bidders flicked their hat brims or sometimes made some almost imperceptible gesture the spotters picked up. Each spotter picked one bidder and that's who he watched for the duration of the sale of this lot. If his buyer bid, the spotter yelled "yo" or "yup" and the auctioneer increased the bid amount. The cadence and words used by the auctioneer always fascinated me. His voice was musical and mesmerizing.

The County Fair 7

Though it wasn't the county seat, the town of Rifle hosted the Garfield County Fair. It was the biggest celebration around, held in late August for the better part of a week and culminating in the weekend activities and rodeos. The Fair certainly had an impact when the Rifle schools decided to open after Labor Day rather than in August. Most of the ranch kids were in 4H so they were busy preparing and showing their 4H projects and wouldn't go to school during the Fair anyway.

We went to the Fair to go to the rodeos but we also spent at least one day looking at all the animals and exhibits. Under the bleachers was where they set up the non-animal exhibits and it was a wonderland. Everything was there for judging so all the ribbons were fun to see. There were home canned goods, baked goods, clothing, flower arrangements, paintings and needle work galore. This is also where all of the non-livestock projects for 4H were displayed and judged such as sewing, cooking, electricity, wildlife, etc. Outdoors at the various sheds and arenas, we saw the sheep, steers, dairy cows, rabbits, pigs, chickens and chinchillas. Sometimes we went up into the grandstands and watched the arena competition such as Western Pleasure or 4H showmanship classes.

We went to town whenever there was a parade or celebration in any of the nearby small towns. Glenwood Springs had Strawberry Days and Carbondale had Potato Days. Later, other towns followed suit with their own town celebrations such as Silt Hey Day and New Castle Burning Mountain Day. These were usually one day affairs, on a Saturday, and the day was full from early morning until way late that night. The day began with a pancake breakfast put on by the local Lions, Moose or Elks clubs or maybe the Chamber of Commerce. Mid morning was the parade. Then there were crafts, exhibits and games for the kids. Families brought picnics for lunch or sometimes there was a concession that sold hot dogs and hamburgers. Vendors, such as there were, always were local groups, often non-profit. There were more activities in the afternoon. The day might end with a rodeo and there was usually live music for dancing.

These celebrations were a chance to get together with friends and neighbors for a visit. Everywhere in town you ran into someone you knew. At any of the town festivities, families often found the same spot year after year, in the shade if possible, to set up lawn chairs and watch all the goings-on in town. In New Castle, at Burning Mountain Day, the Congregational and Episcopal churches went together and sold pie at the Guild Hall. The pies were homemade and delicious. You could buy a whole pie to take home or get a slice and a cup of coffee and eat it in the Guild Hall. You used real dishes, cups (with saucers) and silverware; no plastic or paper here.

We sometimes went for the pancake breakfast but usually for the parade, then went home. There was still ranch work to be done. Some of the summer celebrations in town managed to happen when we were in the middle of haying season. But our goal for second cutting was to be done by the Fair. We didn't always make that goal but were usually pretty close. For the parade, especially the bigger ones in Glenwood or Rifle, we went early to "find a spot." That meant finding a good spot to park as well as a place along the sidewalk where there might be some shade from lilac bushes in people's yards.

For Fair Days, the parade in Rifle went all the way through town on Railroad Avenue, ending at the Fairgrounds. It started with a police car with its lights and siren going, then the Grand Marshal and floats made by all the businesses and clubs in town. People worked on those floats for weeks. It took lots of chicken wire and colored crepe paper. Usually the float was built on somebody's flatbed trailer or hay wagon and often pulled by a tractor. Some floats were pulled by a team of horses. Mr. Cross who owned the jewelry store in Rifle had a really old car (1920s or so) that he had restored and fixed up. It had a sign advertising "FM Cross Jewelers" on the driver's door.

A lot of kids dressed up and rode their decorated bikes in the parade. The Fair and rodeo royalty from all the towns around were dressed up in their western finery and riding horseback. The County Sheriff and his deputies rode horseback. If it was an election year, politicians rode in fancy cars and waved to the crowd while their volunteers handed out bumper stickers. Eight or ten Shriners came up from Grand Junction for our parades. They wore matching shiny yellow and red vests and funny little hats, called a fez, with a tassel on top. The Shriners had tiny little electric cars and entertained the parade crowd by driving in circles, snake shapes and figure eights all along the parade route.

A lot of the floats carried buckets of candy and the riders threw handfuls of candy into the crowd. Under the watchful eye of drivers and parents, kids ran out from the spectators to fill their pockets with candy. A few times, Dad hauled our horses to town and we rode in the parade with other members from our 4H club. You knew the end of the parade was coming when you saw and heard the big red fire truck bringing up the rear.

Besides the parade, 4H events, community exhibits and rodeos, there was a carnival at the Fair. It wasn't very big but had everything you needed including the ferris wheel, scary rides, games of skill and best of all, cotton candy.

We went to at least one of the rodeos over the weekend. On Thursday and Friday nights were the junior rodeos whose participants were teenagers and youngsters from local ranches and clubs. On the weekend was the PRCA rodeos. These cowboys, cowgirls and bullfighters (clowns) were professional rodeo stars that rode the circuit to make a living. Rodeo cowboys are now recognized along with the best athletes in other sports and some make lots of money. Back then, it was a hand to mouth existence and the cowboys did it because they loved it. There were both afternoon and evening pro rodeo performances on

Saturday and Sunday. Walt Alsbaugh, a local contractor, often supplied the bucking stock (bulls and broncs) which was a very big deal for his company and for the County. We usually ate at home but sometimes we got a hamburger and pop (soda) from the concession and joined a packed grandstand crowd to watch the rodeos.

Nothing is more exciting or patriotic than the Grand Entry at a rodeo. All the competitors, judges, royalty, stock contractor and anyone else associated with the rodeo or who happened to have a saddled horse on the fairgrounds gathered on horseback at one end of the arena. Right before the events began, the announcer started some inspirational, patriotic music. I think it was the Stars and Stripes Forever by John Philip Sousa. Everyone stood for the showing of the colors. Led by riders carrying the American flag, Colorado state flag and other pertinent banners, then the Fair royalty and royalty from other nearby county fairs, all the riders rode into the arena single file. Once inside the arena, the pace was as fast as the rider could handle. More accomplished riders got their horses into a full blown run while others galloped, cantered or trotted. The line of horses ran fast and close to the fence around the arena, stopping in a line in the middle of the arena facing the grandstands. Everyone remained standing for the national anthem and then the rodeo began.

The stock events like bull riding, saddle bronc and bareback bronc riding all took place in the big rodeo arena. So did calf roping, steer wrestling and barrel racing. At the same time as those events were going on, there was pole bending and goat tying on the track in front of the grandstands. There was lots to see and hear. Whoever coordinated those rodeos was very good at their job because they usually kept things moving right along and there wasn't much of a time lag between contestants. The chutes where they released the calves for calf roping and the steers for bull dogging were at one end of the arena and the gates where riders came into the arena for barrel racing was at the other end.

The announcer and clerks had a wooden box built in the middle of the bucking chutes and up high. The announcer was like an emcee. He announced contestants, a little about each rider, the name of the bull if they were bull riding and generally kept the audience engaged and amused. He also announced scores or times depending on what event was being run. Judges for scoring the bucking events were out in the arena. The times were kept by timers in a catwalk on the other side of the arena above the grandstands.

Sometime during the rodeo there was a break between events and the clowns would put on an act or there would be a trick riding act or something special to entertain the crowd. Bull riding was always the most popular event and was the grand finale of the rodeo. This is where the clowns, or bull fighters came in. They were very funny and pulled off lots of antics but theirs was the most serious and most dangerous job at the rodeo. Whenever a cowboy was down and defenseless, the bull fighters ran right over to him to distract the bull or bronc and get them away from the cowboy. They were very good at what they did and I never saw a clown get hurt though I know they did. An ambulance was at the Fairgrounds at all times when the rodeos were going on. It was parked outside the arena and there were times when they drove into the arena and took a cowboy or cowgirl to the hospital. At that time, Rifle only had one ambulance so the rodeo would stop until it got back.

When I was very young, my Dad rode bareback and saddle bronc in the rodeos at these events. When he was single, he rode the circuit usually barely winning enough money to pay his entry fees for the next rodeo. Now that he had a young family to support, he only rode at local rodeos. The story goes that once when I was about three and my sister was two, Dad had a bad wreck on a saddle bronc. He got bucked off the bronc but his foot was hung up in the stirrup. Moments later, his foot came out of the boot and all was well. But all of the onlookers, announcer, and family knew it could have been very bad. So for a few seconds, everything was silent. In that dead quiet, my sister yelled out "My Daddy got bucked off!" That broke the tension and everyone laughed.

There weren't any horse races at the Fair but they did have them several weekends in the summer. The race track ran around the outside of the rodeo arena. They even had a fancy starting gate they pulled into place on the track with a really big tractor. When we went to the horse races, I was afraid they wouldn't get the starting gate off the track before the horses came around and there would be a terrible wreck. It never happened but I just knew that tractor was going to die in the middle of the track and they couldn't get it started in time.

≈

Guns were a big part of our lives. We used them to hunt deer and elk for food, shoot varmints like skunks, badgers and porcupines, and put down sick and injured animals. Grandad Cole, Mom's father, was a gunsmith, both Mom and Dad grew up around guns, and guns were a way of life for us. Until we were old enough to shoot for ourselves (eight or nine years old), we girls weren't that interested or excited about guns. They were a normal part of our daily lives and we were taught very early on to have a healthy respect for firearms of all kinds. There were only a few but very important rules:

- Guns are not toys.
- Never, ever touch any gun without permission.
- Never, ever have a loaded gun anywhere near the pickup or the house.
- Even if somebody just checked, when you pick up or are handed a gun, always check for yourself to make sure it's unloaded.
- Never, ever point a gun at another person for any reason. In fact, if you point your gun at something, anything, you better be prepared to shoot.

We learned about guns when we were young and Daddy drilled gun safety into our heads until it was second nature. But I don't remember this lesson to be hard, or even significant in our young lives. We never handled guns unless we had permission and it never entered out minds to disobey. Guns were serious business. We knew Dad trusted us around guns simply because the rules made sense.

Even when we were old enough to take the 22 out without asking explicit permission, we only did that when it was just we girls, not when we had company. We knew Dad thought we were special and visitors to the house, even the adults, might not show the same good sense and maturity that we did. So even when we were little, we felt an added sense of responsibility about Dad's guns when we had company.

Grandad Cole was a skilled gunsmith. Not only did he make, repair and site-in guns, he also reloaded bullets for people in New Castle and half the rest of the county. Actually, he reloaded shells but we called them bullets. The bullet is the tip or projectile made out of lead and copper. Bullets were expensive so once you bought a box or two, you always pocketed the spent shells and kept them to be reloaded. Some of those cardboard shell boxes had been used for so many years they were made more of masking tape than the original cardboard.

Dad learned a lot about reloading, and got much of his equipment from Grandad Cole. He set up the equipment on a workbench in Grandma and Grandad Arthur's barn. We liked to be with Daddy when he was reloading. There were lots of components and steps to the process and an element of danger because of the gunpowder. Daddy measured the powder carefully and as I recall he did a lot of very delicate weighing of both the powder and the lead bullets. Primers came in cute little boxes he let us have to play with when they were empty. There was a small cast iron pot with a pour spout on one end Daddy used to melt lead and make bullets. It was very hot and he was very careful with the tongs he used to tip and pour the lead into molds. The shells were different sizes as were the bullets, depending on the kind and caliber of bullet he was loading.

We had a gun rack in the back window of the pickup that often had one or two rifles in it. So did everybody else in the county. Dad had a 22 pistol under or behind the seat and usually he had his 357 pistol which he tucked into the waistband of his jeans at the small of his back when he got out of the pickup.

Besides hunting for deer and elk with hunting rifles – 22 hornet, 243, 30 ought 6, 30-30, 270 – Dad sometimes shot skunks, porcupines or badgers because they were nuisances on the ranch. He also used a 22 to shoot the lynx he trapped. A few times he had to put down a horse or cow but we girls were always sent to the house when that happened. Once we had a dog that got into Mom's ducks and killed at least one of them. Dad said once a dog got the taste, he couldn't be broken from chasing the livestock and he might teach the other dogs. We couldn't keep the dog. The next day when we got home from school, the dog was gone. I'm sure putting down that dog was one of the hardest things my Dad ever did. He talked tough but he actually had a big, tender heart.

Guns could be fun too, and often were at our house. We spent many summer afternoons and evenings watching Dad and various uncles and adult friends shooting at targets. Outside our front porch and across the small front yard, three or four steps at most, was where we parked the pickup. I can't count the number of times Daddy shot across the hood of the pickup towards the orchard, several dozen yards away. The hood also served as a place to put extra guns, clips, targets and boxes of ammunition. Targets were generally tin or aluminum cans, bottles or paper plates with a black magic marker bull's eye drawn in the center. Real targets were expensive and empty cans were plentiful.

We watched the adults shooting and admired their shots from way behind where the shooting was taking place. No matter how far back and safe we were, Dad always said several times "you kids stay back." After several shots, he would holler at one of us to run out and get what they'd been shooting at and set up new targets.

When it was our turn to shoot, we went through a lot of boxes of 22 long rifle shells. 22 shells were reasonably priced at Bald Bob Sports in Rifle. We loved the plastic boxes with sliding lids and gathered up all the spent shells to use in our pretend games as money or poker chips.

My favorite gun was a 22 with an octagon barrel and flip up site. One reason I liked it was because it was old. Even then I had an interest in and appreciation for family history. Also, that 22 was simple to understand and once I learned how to work the site and the difference between squeezing and pulling the trigger I got to be a pretty good shot. It was a lot of fun. I'm not sure it was true but Dad liked to say I was a better shot with that old 22 single shot than most boys were with their fancy 22s.

As much fun as shooting was getting the cans afterwards, checking out the hits and misses, then setting up more cans. We learned more about guns and shooting that way than you could learn in a dozen classroom lessons. Besides target shooting on the ranch, whenever we were up country somewhere, Mom and Dad would pull the pickup over and we'd shoot, or watch Dad shoot. There are several spots around the Rhubarb Patch, Willow Creek and Reservoir Park where we could probably still find lead or spent 22 shells from years ago.

One time during high water in the spring, I don't know who was at the house but I imagine it was probably Uncle Ernie and the Whitman clan. Dad and Uncle Ernie decided to have we kids throw empty pop and beer cans in the creek on the upper side of the bridge. Then they waited until the cans floated out from under the bridge on the other side and shot them until they were full of holes and sank. We all thought it was a lot of fun.

In seventh grade, we were required to take a two day hunter's safety course. When you passed the class, you got a card that allowed you to buy a hunting license in Colorado. It was fun to show up all those town boys on the shooting part of the test when I got one of the highest scores for accuracy.

High Water 8

Work on the ranch never let up but it did change with the seasons. Winter was a time to feed the hay we grew. Early in the spring, the calves were born. Later in the spring, when the snow melted in the high country, we irrigated the hayfields. Early summer we branded and moved the cattle to the upper pasture. Mid and late summer we put up the hay. Fall was for canning and hunting season. And the cycle began again.

In the winter, we moved the cows to the hayfields, leaving the gates open between them, usually near a haystack where it was convenient. We fed near the creek so there was fresh water. In especially cold winters, the creek froze over each night and we took an axe to open it up again for the cows in the morning. Even if some of the cows had wandered away looking for fresh grass, they would all be back in the morning to get fed. Dad put chains on the tires of both of our tractors with the first blizzard of the winter and they stayed on through mud season in the spring. So in low gear, they could go almost anywhere regardless of the conditions.

I think we figured it was one bale of hay to three or four cows depending on how much cold weather and snow there was. It was especially important that heavy (pregnant) cows got plenty of feed for them and the calf they were carrying. The hay was loaded from the haystack onto the wagon. It was a two person job, one for driving and one for doing the feeding, but sometimes one person fed, putting the tractor in its lowest gear and heading it off across the field.

Fields were often rutted so it could be quite a balancing act standing on the wagon and getting the twine cut. Feeding involved cutting the two strands of twine on each bale so you always kept your pocket knife handy. Then you'd flake off a wedge of hay four or five inches thick and push it off onto the ground. You needed to keep up the pace of throwing the hay off the wagon because you wanted the hay spread out a bit but not all the way across the field.

We also fed a supplement called alfalfa pellets that were made of compressed alfalfa, minerals and other nutrients. The pellets were made at Valley Farms pellet mill in Silt. I think McPhersons, among others, were involved in the operation. We also kept a salt block near where we fed. The cows followed along waiting for you to start kicking out the hay and some of the most curious stuck their noses up on the wagon while you were trying to get it thrown off. Cows can be big babies sometimes, annoyingly stubborn at others, and are always entertaining.

We threw all the twine in a pile near the haystack. We always needed baling twine on the ranch. Then we closed up the haystack by pulling the deer fence back around and wiring it. We fed in the same tracks until it started to get rutted and packed down, then the next day we'd move a bit and feed in a different spot.

Even though the hayfields were out in the open, we made sure the cows also had access to cedar covered hillsides so they could bed down out of the elements. Generally you don't want cows feeding in the alfalfa fields because they'll eat too much green alfalfa, bloat and die. In winter, the alfalfa wasn't growing and the hayfields were covered with snow so it was okay to feed there. Feeding was another one of the many ranch chores that had to be done "come rain or shine," "in sickness or in health." If you had cows and horses, or other livestock, they had to be fed. Every day. You couldn't take the day off because you were sick, tired, didn't feel like doing it, bad weather or any other reason.

In the spring when the snow melted, the whole ranch seemed to be made of mud. Often it was deep enough to go over your boots and half way up your calf. And a lot of the time, it wasn't mud, but mud mixed with manure. Mud everywhere and Mom did her best to keep it out of the house. Almost daily, I was out on the porch with a stick scraping the mud off the bottom of my shoes.

Dad and Grandad never wore any other shoes except their cowboy boots. They had rubber overshoes with metal buckles that fit the shape of the boots and were taller than the boot. The overshoes were easy to maintain by rinsing them off in the creek or with the outside hose at Grandma and Grandad's house. Then they were propped upside down near the stove to dry inside and out and ready to wear next time you needed them.

Also in the spring, we harrowed. No particular person did this job, just whoever was available. I know Mom spent a lot of hours driving the tractor and pulling the harrow back and forth across the fields. Wherever the horses and cows were kept over the winter would be a winter's worth of manure. Cow manure is good, rich fertilizer. Horse manure is as well, in small quantities, but it's too rich for flower beds and vegetable gardens. To break up the manure and spread it out around the field, we pulled a harrow behind the tractor. Harrowing also loosens up the dirt so the alfalfa and grass grow better.

Our harrow was a series of chains laying flat on the ground and bars full of short metal teeth. The harrow is attached to the tractor with a logging chain. Mom tells of bringing the harrow back from over the hill and knocking off a lot of the teeth on the rocky road. She had to stop the tractor, walk back and pick up all the parts so they could repair the harrow for the next field.

In the spring, we moved the mother cows about ready to calve from the hayfields into the cedars. We usually calved at the Jones' place or over the hill at Grandma and Grandad's. Ranchers know all of their livestock and Daddy could tell when a cow was in distress or might be soon. So those were watched closely. We checked on them at least once a day, more often if a cow showed signs of problems. First-calf heifers were especially susceptible to having trouble birthing. If the cow was having trouble, Daddy could pull the calf and both cow and calf would be okay.

When he called a vet to come out, we knew it was serious. The veterinarian did his best to come to the ranch quickly because time could mean the difference between life and death for both the cow and calf.

There were several good vets in the area. In pre-cell phone times, vets kept in contact with their offices by phone if the ranch they were on had one. A few had short wave radios in their pickups. If we were lucky, one of the vets would be at some other ranch nearby. Losing a cow and calf was a big deal on the ranch. Not only would we miss the monetary loss in production capability but also because we were sad when one of our animals died. Even though they weren't pets, they were still like part of the family.

There is nothing cuter than a baby Hereford calf with its reddish brown hair and white face, bleating for its mother. We kids were warned about separating a mother cow from her calf. A mother cow protecting her young is nothing to mess with. She's 1000 pounds of hooves, snot and bulk, and madder than mad. So we usually watched the babies and laughed at their antics from a safe distance. There were exceptions, especially during branding and when we moved the cows and calves up country that we got more up close and personal with both the cows and calves.

Grandad vaccinated the calves right after they were born but sometimes they got sick anyway and you could tell right away by the color of their diarrhea. I'll always remember calf scour green. Especially when Dad and Grandad would have it all over their boots and jeans while they wrestled with a calf to give it a shot of penicillin. Our family still uses that phrase to describe cars and other things of a similar obnoxious color and we laugh.

When one of our horses was about ready to drop a foal, Dad often moved her into our yard, in case she had trouble. But then he left her alone and we checked on her off and on. We girls kept watch from the living room window. I think he had to help a mare a time or two but I don't remember having to call a vet when the horses gave birth. If we were lucky, we had two or three colts per year. That's about all the young horses Dad could break and still put in full days doing other ranch work.

≈

As days got warmer and snow started to melt in the high country, the ice on the creek melted and the water rose.

The creek was mesmerizing, especially to children. It was mysterious and a little scary. In fact, there were times when it was a lot scary. Sometimes during spring runoff, the creek rose many feet and overflowed its banks. Usually it rose significantly but gradually as the snow melted high in the mountains. But if there was a particularly warm day, a gently babbling brook turned into a thunderous, broiling mass of water in just a few minutes. The sheer power of the creek was evident in the way the water came roaring and tumbling along its way, carrying with it everything in its path. High water usually only lasted a few days or up to a couple of weeks and it was both fascinating and terrifying. Some years were worse than others and bridges would be washed out all up and down the creek.

Most of the ranches along Divide Creek had property on both sides of the creek so had at least one bridge. We had three bridges on our place. Our bridges were made of two large logs laid side by side spanning the creek and planks. The bridges at our house and at the Jones Place were built where there was a drop off of about 15 feet from the bank to the creek on both sides. I'm sure whoever put in the first bridges dug it out on both sides of the creek so the bridge could be secured properly. The bridge at Grandma and Grandad's house was only a few feet off the water. As high water came down the creek, we checked often to see if there were any big logs or trees that might cause a problem with the bridge. If there would have been, I don't know what we were going to do about it besides watch disaster happen. I don't remember any of our bridges washing out although there were times when there was no clearance between the water and the bottom of the bridge.

When there had been a long winter and heavy snowpack in the mountains, high water scoured the creek banks for miles. Any branches or trees that had fallen into the creek since the last high water came roaring down the creek with all the mud and water. Usually it was one of these big trees that lodged itself in the bank or under the bridge creating a temporary dam. When the dam broke, away went the bridge.

Those years, besides rebuilding bridges, headgates usually needed serious repair as well. Maintenance of the headgates and ditches were always a chore in the spring. One time, during high water, just to make the whole thing more exciting, Daddy decided to build a dam with a big, almost dead cottonwood tree near the headgate of the King Ditch. The King ditch started just down the creek from our house. The creek had washed around the headgate and no water was going down the ditch. I don't remember if it was already down or they cut it down but Daddy and Uncle Ernie managed to get a big cottonwood log into the creek. So far so good. But the current was a bit quicker than they thought it was and the tree headed down the creek. It looked like it was going to go right past the ditch, around the corner and on down the creek where it could potentially create havoc by blocking the creek where we didn't want it.

Dad hollered for a rope so someone brought him a lariat. He snagged the end of the log like he was roping a calf. The rope gave him enough leverage to maneuver the log to where he wanted it. They got one end of the log wedged into the creek bank and bulled the other end around to the opposite side of the creek and tied it off with the rope. Perfect. Except the rope was Daddy's best, favorite, most expensive lariat. No one ever admitted who it was that went and got the rope.

Besides working on headgates, ditches had to be walked and cleaned. Usually it just took some heavy lifting to move rocks and shovel out dirt that had fallen into the ditch over the winter. Sometimes the whole bank of the ditch gave way requiring a bulldozer or backhoe. If a boulder was too big to move by hand but not enough trouble to hire a bulldozer fell into the ditch, Dad had a solution – dynamite. In those days, you could buy sticks or half-sticks of dynamite at the local feed store or hardware store. Dad was careful and made sure everything and everyone was safe but I think he really got a kick out of blowing a big rock to smithereens.

The King-Heatherly ditch headgate was about a mile above our house. The hillside between our place and the headgate was very steep. The ditch washed out often. When that happened, Dad came back from irrigating and told Mom he had no water. They'd grab a bunch of gunnysacks and walk up the ditch. Sometimes they walked a long way until they found the washout where all the water was running down the hill. They filled dozens and dozens of gunny sacks with dirt and threw them down in the hole. Dad jumped and stomped on them to pack them in, then threw in some more gunnysacks of dirt until it finally stopped the washout and the water was going down the ditch again.

There was one place where the ditch crossed a gully. They built a wooden culvert and put it in across the gully. It took lots of repairs. They lined the culvert with visquine (heavy black plastic) using big headed nails to tack it down. It worked pretty well and lasted until the plastic rotted every year and then they did it again. As Mom said, "that's what you get with a nickel and dime operation."

Once when they needed to work on the headgate or the ditch, they drove up the road above our house to a spot where a big cottonwood tree had fallen across the creek. Dad walked right on across it with his shovel and gunnysacks. Mom wasn't happy about it but she got across the log too with Dad walking backwards and sticking the shovel into the log for her to hold onto. When they were done fixing the ditch, Dad went back across the log and drove home. Mom walked the ditch. After that, no matter how far it was, she always walked the ditch.

The difference between a normal high water year and an especially nasty one was the amount of snow over the winter and duration of the runoff. If it was a particularly warm spring and the snow melted all at once, all that water came down the creek in a matter of days. If the days were warm but the evenings still cool in the mountains, the snow melted more slowly and the runoff lasted a couple of weeks with less destruction in its path.

Even during high water, the creek often seemed almost normal in the evenings. But Mom still wouldn't let us go down to the creek to play. She explained the snow melted during the day, then slowed down melting during the nights which were still very cold in the high country. The high water had quite a distance to travel so usually hit the lower country, where the ranches and Colorado River were, in the middle of the night or early morning hours. We also learned that like a gully washer, the water would come up much faster than you expected. So the creek was off limits during the whole time there was high water.

Every year after high water, when Mom let us play near the creek again, we loved exploring and checking out all our favorite places for new things. Each year, the creek changed in subtle ways. Some places were eroded away, other silted in. It was amazing what the creek brought down and deposited as driftwood. Besides interesting gnarled tree roots, there were huge logs and lots of branches. We found quakie logs that had been stripped of bark and gnawed down by beavers. We always wondered what poor beaver had his dam and home swept out from under him. Sometimes we found parts of boards and wondered where they came from. One year a huge pile of driftwood piled up against one curve in the creek and we spent all summer looking through it for treasure and climbing all over it for fun.

Above the Jones' Place, the creek made a beautiful horseshoe bend. Every year, the horseshoe changed until one year, taking the most direct route down country, the creek cut through and bypassed the horseshoe bend entirely. It was quite impressive and a significant event in our lives on the ranch.

We depended entirely on the spring runoff for irrigation water so when the snow melt was about done and creek levels fell below headgates, we were done irrigating. Therefore we only got two cuttings of hay and irrigated only for the first where those farmers down by the Colorado River got three, sometimes four cuttings.

Three ditches provided our irrigation water: the King-Heatherly, the King and June Creek. The headgate to the King-Heatherly, which we called the Big Ditch, was above our house. The headgate to the King ditch was at the house and the June Creek ditch came out of June Creek. The King ditch ended up at Hall's place where he had some shares of water.

Many times I remember Dad griping about our neighbor down the creek, stealing water. He was convinced that when no one was around, Mr. Hall changed the weir so more water went his way. There were also confrontations where Mom just knew Dad's Irish temper was going to get the best of him, he'd bop Mr. Hall with the shovel – or shoot him with the 357. Dad was a lot of blunder but I don't think anyone wanted to call his bluff.

Ditches had to be built so you could move the irrigation water where you wanted it without going up a hill. It seems obvious water can't run up hill so the ditch had to handle that limitation. Considering the length of our ditches, the miles and miles the water had to travel, and the fact that we lived in the mountains must have made ditch surveying and engineering no small accomplishment. One of Dad's biggest complements was that "so and so could make water run uphill".

Placement and angle of the headgate in the creek was crucial. It needed to be positioned so just the right amount of water went into the ditch. If the ditch and headgate was aimed straight into the creek, you wouldn't get enough water in the ditch. If it was angled too sharply up-creek, you'd get too much water and it would probably wash around the headgate or wash it out altogether. Either way, you didn't get water in the ditch. Even if you did get the headgate just right, it would probably wash out during high water the following spring and you'd have to start over anyway.

Our headgates and weirs were made of metal or wood or a combination of the two. Inevitably, the creek washed dirt and gravel away from the headgate, jeopardizing that part of the ditch as well as making sure that water didn't get into the ditch. Dad used anything available to stuff in the washed out places around the headgate. You were likely to find boards, big rocks and sandbags packed in with the dirt around the headgates. No matter what you did to make a headgate work, it involved lots and lots of shoveling. To manage how much water went in the ditch, the headgate or weir had removable boards to adjust amounts of water.

I don't pretend to understand water adjudication now and I certainly didn't then. In the practical sense, our ranch owned a certain number of shares of water from East Divide Creek, as did all the other farms and ranches on the creek. In good years, everybody got their full shares of water. In dry years, I believe senior shares (older) came first and the newer allotments came last so might not get all the water they needed or were due. At any rate, there's never enough water in western Colorado.

Headgates in the creek measured the amount of water going into the ditches. Weirs in the ditches measured the allotment of water to each property. Water for irrigation is measured in acre-feet. An acre-foot is the amount of water it takes to cover one acre to a depth of one foot. It's a visual thing because I can never remember how many gallons that is. Nor does it matter. All of that is an extreme over simplification of a very complex and controversial (often litigated) concept. The history of the west is built on wars over water and it still happens today, especially in the Colorado River drainage where the river is so over adjudicated that people own many more water shares than water is actually available even in good, wet years.

Besides our water shares from East Divide Creek, the ranch also got all the water from June Creek. Less than half a mile up the road from the Big Ditch headgate, you took a left and drove down the hill, across East Divide Creek when the water was low and up the June Creek Road. This road was dirt, four wheel drive on the best of days, narrow, and rutted. Actually, it was more of a trail than a road. It went on into the high country for many miles, first dropping over into what we called the Basin.

Long before it reached The Basin, in fact a short ways up the hill from East Divide Creek, the trail began to follow June Creek which drained into East Divide Creek. Shortly after that, it crossed a ditch. During high water we diverted June Creek into this ditch. I'm not sure it even required a headgate, June Creek was such a small stream. And it was named for the obvious, June Creek only ran until June.

The Big Ditch ran above the horse pasture above our house. Dad used a piece of large rubber hose to siphon water from the big ditch into a feeder ditch to water the horse pasture. In the top corner of the horse pasture, the big ditch had a low spot where we drove across to get up into the hayfields.

Irrigating our hayfields and pastures was all about getting the water spread across the field and soaked evenly. We didn't use fancy piping or tarpaulin dams to move the water around. It was just man and shovel against water. With years of doing the work, Daddy and Grandad knew about how much water one man could chase each day. So fields were irrigated in sections. Their irrigating boots were knee high or above-the-knee rubber boots and Dad made sure his shovel was sharp before irrigating started. To get water from the ditch, a nice big chunk of sod and mud was cut out in a v-shape, less than the width of the shovel. Usually that chunk was immediately used to block water in another place. Watching my dad irrigate, he had a methodological approach that almost seemed rhythmic. Slice out a shovel full of mud and sod, toss it firmly into another place. Redo as many times as it took to get the job done. Tiny ditches were sliced perpendicular to the ditch to get the water headed down through the field.

In this way, sections of each field were watered in succession. Irrigating was done both morning and evening, seven days a week, so water got moved twice a day. I don't know how they divided up the irrigating but Dad and Grandad had their own parts of the over 450 acres we irrigated on the ranch. Once either of them got all the fields and pastures irrigated on their side, they'd start again and keep irrigating until there was no more water. I'm sure if there had been an over abundance of water, they would have known when to stop irrigating. But that never happened. The creek got low and the ditches ran dry first.

As the alfalfa and wild grasses grew in the fields, by the time the hay was ready to cut, the fields were dry enough to drive through without getting the machinery stuck in the mud or digging ruts. The rest of the year, the only moisture came from the few rains we got in our semi-arid climate.

≈

We had lots of adventures going with Dad and Grandad to irrigate. I'm told I cured Grandad of cursing all together. Apparently, I was helping Grandad irrigate the hayfields. This mostly involved me playing in the mud and getting as wet and dirty as possible. As Grandad used his shovel to move chunks of dirt to allow water down one part of the field and stop it from spreading over the rest of the field, a snake made a surprise appearance. I don't know if it was a big bull snake or a smaller water snake.

Both had important jobs on the ranch. Water snakes eat insects and otherwise mind their own business. Dark brown or gray, they're hardly ever more than a foot long and as big around as your little finger. Bull snakes are much bigger, several feet long and several inches around. They're dark yellow with big brown spots and love to eat moles, field mice and other small critters. Bull snakes are important on the ranch because many of the varmints they eat burrow and dig holes in the hayfields. It's not funny when you see the irrigation water you've so carefully spread out over a hayfield go right down a hole and reappear fifty or so feet farther down in the field. Needless to say, you won't get much hay off that dry spot. You didn't have to like the snakes but you had to tolerate them. I personally liked to play with snakes. This was partly because I knew everyone else in my family avoided snakes at all cost.

At any rate, this snake surprised Grandad. At dinner that night, his four year old granddaughter (me) reported I had fun except for being surprised by the "goddamn snake". No one heard Grandad cuss ever again.

Another time, the four of us were all walking from the bridge up to the house. When we got to the garden, a huge bull snake was stretched completely across the road in front of us. This thing had to be six feet long and six inches in diameter. Well, it seemed like six. Mom says it was more like four inches around. In this case, no one was surprised by the snake but no one was particularly thrilled to see him either. Following our rule of respecting them and leaving them alone, we simply climbed up the hill a bit and walked around the snake (way, way around) and let him go on about his business.

Moving Cows   9

About the same time of year we were irrigating was when we branded. It took a day or two to gather all the cows from the fields and pastures where they had spent the winter. We fenced them in along the creek bottom down by our sheds and corral. It was inevitable some cows and their calves got separated so the night before we branded, it was very noisy when all the cows were bawling for their babies all night long.

We used the corral for ear-tagging, vaccinating and branding the new calves for that year, and castrating and dehorning the bull calves. Dad's brand was Lazy Open A Quarter Circle Bar $\subset\!\!\leftarrow$ but we used Grandad's brand, Lazy H, Inverted T $\perp$. Because it could be made with a single straight branding iron, it was simple and convenient. It was easier to make the brand by just burning the hair. Fancier branding irons and less skilled cowboys tended to smudge the brand and make huge sores and scabs if the calf's skin was burned. We also had a smaller iron for horses that was the lazy H inverted T brand on one iron. Happily, the brand is still in the family. After the ranch was sold, Mom and Daddy kept the brand. Then Tammi and Roger Whitaker, her husband, have kept it current all these years.

The day or so after the cows and calves were gathered, we branded and everybody helped. If we weren't helping, we all hung on the corral poles to watch. Usually Uncle Ernie and Uncle Steve and families came to help branding so it was great fun for us to have all our cousins around.

They built a little fire in the corral and let it burn down to coals to heat the branding irons. It was fascinating to watch Grandad gather all the paraphernalia he needed. There were vials of vaccine, syringes, the eartag machine (it looked sort of like a pair of pliers), and the burner to sear the calves' horns.

We separated the cows from their calves and put the calves in the corral. Now it got really noisy with those cows bawling for their babies. One guy roped a calf and walked/drug it over to the fire and sort of sat on its shoulders/head. Someone else held its feet. Dad branded while Grandad did his thing with the vaccine and eartag. They castrated the bull calves and it was all usually done in short order. The calf was turned out with the cows and the whole thing repeated until all the calves were done. It took all morning, a stop for dinner, and all afternoon.

We girls practiced roping all year long and one year, Dad finally let us help by having us rope the calves for them during branding. I think we were 8 or 9 years old. We were so excited and had so much fun. Our cousin, Bobby, Tammi and I ran around the corral, each with a lariat. When we caught a calf, we'd pull the loop tight and then drop the rope. When they needed another calf to brand, they brought us another rope and grabbed a rope with a calf on it. We caught the calves but we also spent a lot of time messing around, trying to lead them around the corral. Best of all, the grownups treated us like were part of the crew and told us how much help we were.

Blisters, scrapes and scratches were common on the ranch. If you did much shoveling, you'd get blisters on your hands. Riding, you could get blisters on the insides of your thighs. Much walking in boots made blisters on heels. Some of the worst blisters I ever had were rope burns on the palms of my hands.

Other times, you did not want to let go of the rope. Especially when Mom or Dad said to "hold onto that and don't let it go." When we were told to do anything, we generally didn't need to be told twice. Even though we were kids, sometimes our helping and working together as a family meant the difference between getting the job done or making it drag out while Mom and Dad did it without us

Sometimes a sick cow or steer had to be roped to be doctored. Dad always did that but we loved to practice roping from horseback just in case. Also, sometimes Dad roped us for fun. Well, fun for him anyway. When we practiced roping, we learned to use the saddle horn. If you caught a calf out on the ranch and let the rope go, you might chase it all day to get the rope back. Trying to hold the lariat with a bucking, kicking, running calf on the other end meant rope burns on your hands. But that's what the saddle horn was for. As soon as you catch the calf, you dally the end of the rope around the saddle horn three or four times and then the horse does the work.

When a calf took off across the flat at the pasture and somebody took off on their horse to head it off, very rarely would we get the calf turned before it had gone barreling out into the bushes. I swear it's true that a calf can outrun a horse any day.

≈

A day or two after branding, we trailed the Hereford cows, calves and bulls, and Holsteins seven miles up to our high country pasture for the summer. Trailing cows means they walked up the road and we rode horseback in the rear to push them. Our high country property was called the Moore place or the upper place but we generally just called it the pasture.

Moving cows to the pasture was planned days in advance and was an all day trip. We never did it on a weekend if it could be avoided because there was more traffic. When a car or pickup showed up, they eased their way along and the cows got out of the way. Once in awhile, it would be someone who'd never gone through a herd before or didn't care and they revved their engines and honked which set off my Dad's Irish. Then one of us rode slowly through the cows directly in front of the car, hoping the driver wouldn't hit our horse.

If some of the cows started running up or down the road, we'd slow them down again before they all started running. Sometimes it was a bit of a challenge to get ahead of that first cow or calf and get them turned. The last thing we wanted was a bunch of worn out and upset cows and calves all because of an ignorant or insensitive driver. In those days, we usually only met two or three cars all day and it was usually some other rancher or someone we knew from town who was going up-country fishing.

Someone rode or drove in the lead of the herd then, when we got close, went on up to the pasture to get the gate. Keeping the herd moving wasn't a problem because our Holsteins took the lead and headed for the pasture with a purpose. They'd been there before and knew what awaited them. We took the Holsteins that weren't currently being milked to the upper pasture so they could be in with the bulls and get bred. The upper pasture had good feed, plenty of water, and was cooler in the summer than the rest of the ranch.

Most of the trip had barbed wire fences on both sides of the road. At least two or three calves crawled through the fence every time we moved cows. When they figured out they really didn't want to be on the other side of the fence, they followed along with the herd and usually got back through the fence. If they didn't, we kids got off our horses and climbed through the fence. Eventually we got the calf back on the right side of the fence and hurried to get our horses from Mom and catch up with the herd.

If you were in the lead, you closed open gates or stood in broken fences until the cows went by. Patience was a virtue because in some cases, you might be waiting quite awhile. When we arrived at the pasture, the people in the lead opened the gate to the pasture, then stood in the middle of the road and turned the cows in.

Dad and we girls rode horseback at the tail end of the herd. We pushed along any stragglers and retrieved any calves that might have gone through the fence and not returned to its mother. Calves that just couldn't make the trip and laid down alongside the road were picked up and put in the back of the pickup Mom was driving. The trick is to let the cows move along at their own pace. But if they got distracted by some green grass, we'd go move that cow on up the road before they all decided to follow her and take a break. We also didn't want to fuss with them too much and get them upset and running or milling around. Slow but steady was the way to get the job done.

By noontime, we were hungry and happy to see the sandwiches, apples, chips and homemade cookies Mom brought. She also had jugs of water and koolaid. Riding behind the cows was hot, dusty business. We wore jeans, boots, long sleeved shirts and hats. Anytime we were near the creek, the horse and I both drank. No matter how hot it was, we always wore long sleeves to protect our arms from sunburn and from nasty scratches you might get crawling through bushes and barbed wire fences chasing baby calves. Sometimes as we rode along, we tied our long sleeved shirts to the saddle horn and just wore our tank tops or T-shirts.

Before moving the cows up country, we fixed fence, put out salt blocks and fixed the water supply. The biggest part of the pasture was on the west side of the road. It had a small spring but the spring didn't produce enough water for the cows. The creek went through the smaller part of our pasture on the other side of the road. To get water to the cows, we had a two inch pipe stuck in the creek above the cabin. The pipe went under the road and ran into a big metal water tank out in the pasture. It was gravity driven and worked well. Sometimes it worked too well, the water tank overflowed and it made several inches of mud and manure around the tank. From walking around in this muck every day, some of the cows got foot rot. It was a serious condition if not treated immediately, but with treatment, and getting the sick cow out of the mud, they recovered.

Later in the summer, we moved the cows across the road to the smaller pasture and let them graze it for a few days before we gathered them and trailed them back home. There was a marshy spot near the creek that was always full of reeds and cattails. For some reason, the Holsteins were attracted to the bog. I guess the greenery looked tasty. One time one of the cows was up to her knees in the marsh, looking around and happily chewing her cud. We hollered, yelled and threw rocks, sticks and whatever else we could get our hands on. She just stood there and looked at us. Eventually, Grandma had to go in and chase her out of the bog and back up on higher, and drier, ground.

Though it was only seven miles between our house and the pasture, the altitude changed quite a bit. We lived in the foothills with cedars, pinon, oakbrush and sagebrush. The pasture was truly in the mountains with spruce, pine, elk brush (mountain mahogany) and quaking Aspen trees. In fact, as we drove up country, our pasture at around 6500 feet in elevation was where the quakies really started growing.

≈

There was a little sawmill on the ranch. It and a stack yard were between Grandma and Grandad's house and the gate into the Thirteen Acres. When we referred to that part of the place, we just called it the sawmill. I think the sawmill was one of Dad, Uncle Steve and Uncle Ernie's grand schemes to make some money.

One summer, when we were 5 or 6 years old, Daddy and Uncle Ernie cut trees above Reservoir Park and hauled them down to the sawmill at Grandma and Grandad's where they cut the logs for the cabin. After they cut the logs at the sawmill, they hauled them with tractor and wagon back up country to our upper pasture. We loved it because after they got part way to the pasture, they let us ride on top of the load of logs.

The next summer we built our cabin on the creek side of the pasture, surrounded by tall spruce trees. Mom, Dad, Grandma and Grandad built the cabin by hand in addition to doing the regular ranch work. We kids spent hours hauling mud for chinking the logs. The dirt down by the creek was very sandy and wouldn't stick between the logs. But we knew where there was good mud. We took our pails across the road to the water tank and filled them from the mud around the tank. We were happily caulking the chinks when Mom came around the corner to check on us and from the overwhelming smell, she could tell what we'd done. In our defense, the mud and manure mixture stuck really good! Grandad told us it was okay and it wouldn't smell so bad after it dried.

The cabin sat on a foundation made of rocks which we hauled from the creek. It was made of logs about six inches in diameter which had been cut to fit together like Lincoln logs. It had a sturdy board roof with green roofing on top. The cabin was one room about twenty foot square. It had a wood floor, door and two windows. We furnished the cabin with bunkbeds, box springs and a wood burning stove in one corner with a stovepipe that went through the roof. As a cupboard, an old wooden pannier was nailed to the wall. Grandad Cole built and used this heavy pannier for packing during hunting and camping trips. It must have been a strong horse or donkey that carried two of these panniers. The front of it was hinged and propped up by an attached board as a leg, creating a counter. It had many drawers and cubbies where dishes, silverware, spices, canned goods and other things could be stored. It was so well built that it was mouse proof.

There were at least three wood burning cook stoves used by the ranch: our house, the cabin at the Moore place and the one we used for hunting camp. When I was a kid, they were easy to come by because as people moved to gas and electric ranges, they generally had no use for their old cook stoves. Now they're antiques and cost thousands of dollars more than they did when they were new.

There was a big spruce tree next to the cabin. We built roads and tunnels in the dirt, pine cones and pine needles where we played with our matchbox cars. We also liked to play in the middle of the road where the silt was inches deep. It was the softest dirt we'd ever felt.

Lots of hard work and long hours are involved in keeping a cattle ranch going. But there was also time spent waiting for something to happen or get done. One of those times, Grandma was sitting on the only rock in the meadow by the road at the upper pasture. Maybe she was waiting for someone to move some cows so she could get the gate. Maybe she was just resting.

She saw a shiny rock so she bent over and picked it up. It was green agate and turned out to be a scraper – something the Utes would have used to flesh out deer or elk hides. We often found chips and partial arrowheads on our ranch as it was in the middle of what had been the Ute winter camping grounds. Grandma's scraper was a real find.

The girls
on Ole Paint.

The girls
getting ready for
a ride.

Bobby,
Kathleen,
Tammi and
Johnny on
Tony.

Grandma and
Grandad in front of
their house.

The four of us
in Grandma
and
Grandad's
yard.

Dad and Mom,
icicles on the
side of our house.

Crown Point above our Herefords at the pasture.

Building the cabin at the pasture.
Mom on the roof. Grandad on ladder and
the girls helping by holding the ladder.

The red 1948 GMC pickup.

The barnyard including granary and
homestead cabin (upper right).

The new cinder block barn, finished 1952.

Bobby, Dad on stack. Aunt Nancy, Uncle Steve and Grandad on slip.

Uncle Steve, Tammi, Bobby, Kathleen, Grandad and Dad.

Cows and horses waiting to be fed on a cold winter morning.

Mom, Aunt Ruthie,
kids and dog
catching a ride on the
hay wagon.

Dad and Kathleen on
stack, Grandad
on wagon.

The haystack, the elevator
and the crew.

Dad, Alan Hammontree, Uncle Ernie and Aunt Nancy

Dehorning.

Branding.

Grandad getting ready to vaccinate the calves.

Lynx.

The girls
skinning a beaver to
earn spending money.

Kathleen and Tammi
on the double-track
snow-machine.

Haying Season   10

The 450 acres of alfalfa fields on our ranch were in three areas on the place, or that's how I thought of them anyway. There were the hayfields above our house and at the Jones' place. The second area was the fields by Grandma and Grandad's house and across the creek. The third was the two big hayfields over the hill from Grandma and Grandad's. All of the hayfields except those at Grandma and Grandad's were built on sloping hillsides, some more steep than others, and had to be irrigated during the few weeks in the spring when there was enough water to run through our ditches. Our hay was alfalfa and a combination of timothy, orchard and brome grasses. The hay had to be put up when the grass and alfalfa was ready and at its most nutritious. Haying season couldn't be planned or postponed. According to the ripeness of grass and alfalfa and suitable weather conditions, when it was time to put up the hay, everybody stopped what they were doing and we put up the hay. The ranch had no hired hands so when something big was happening, like putting up the hay, we all became ranch hands and field workers. Even Grandma Arthur who didn't drive a car would often drive the tractor.

Before haying season, Dad and Grandad pulled each piece of equipment down to the barn, greased everything that needed it and made sure everything was in good working order. We generally grew enough hay on the ranch each year to feed our herd of Herefords, the horses and the milk cows. There wasn't any leftover to sell and we usually didn't need to buy any.

They grew barley on the ranch at one time to feed the pigs but Grandad was allergic to it. The emphysema he'd contracted from his years blacksmithing in the gold mines over by Cripple Creek was made worse by the barley. So all of our fields were in alfalfa and grass for hay. For a couple of years, we tried to grow hay grazer. Hay grazer was the latest and greatest in nutritional supplements for cattle. Across the creek from the Thirteen Acres and down the creek from the Jones' place, they cleared the sagebrush from a fairly flat spot. The ditch went directly above the new field and that's where they planted the hay grazer.

It grew tall and had stalks and leaves that looked a lot like corn. We tried cutting and baling it but it wasn't good feed after it dried so we pastured it off. The nutritional benefits for our small herd of cows wasn't worth the cost or hassle so after a couple of years, we didn't grow the hay grazer anymore.

Alfalfa hay is an excellent feed for cattle, especially to sustain them through long, cold Colorado winters. An odd thing though, hay was very good and nutritious for cows but alfalfa standing green in the field could be deadly. If the cows ever got out in the hayfields before the first frost in the fall, everyone hurried to get them back out. Green alfalfa makes cows bloat up because their complex digestive systems can't handle the rich protein. Oddly enough, green alfalfa doesn't bother horses at all.

It was steady work from the time Daddy started cutting the first field until the last bale was in a haystack. There was no taking the day off unless it rained, which we always hoped wouldn't happen because too much rain could ruin the crop. Our alfalfa fields had been planted many years ago and were probably in need of a replanting. So the alfalfa grew to about knee high, in a good year. I think we re-seeded a hayfield only once or twice the entire time I was growing up. It was expensive to buy the alfalfa seed and time consuming to plow, disk and plant.

The alfalfa only grew once each summer so our first cutting was alfalfa and grass. As a rule, Dad and Grandad tried to be done with first cutting by the Fourth of July. Second cutting was mostly grass and we tried to have it put up by Fair Days at the end of August. Dad said the hay was ready to cut when the alfalfa was in about one third bloom. That means, if you looked across an alfalfa field, about one third of the plants would be blooming. A field in full bloom wasn't so great because the hay was past its most nutritious. Either way, the pink and violet fields sure looked pretty.

Dad first opened each hayfield by using the swather to mow two windrows around the outside of the field. This gave him space to turn the swather around because the rest of the field was swathed in straight rows. A windrow is hay the width that a baler can pick up, maybe two or three feet wide and was formed as the rake on the swather snagged the cut hay lying flat on the ground and pulled it together into a narrow row of hay that started at one end of the field and ended at the other. The rake was as wide as the swather and as tall as a kid. It turned on an axis so the long rows of tines went round and round. Think of a water wheel that is about twelve feet wide and six feet in diameter with raking tines instead of water containers.

The mowing part of the swather, or the sickle, was made up of dozens of sharp, triangular blades about 3" by 3" bolted into a metal bar. They looked like tiny grayish-silver Christmas trees to me. The blades moved rapidly back and forth to cut the hay. Sometimes, the blades got broken or worn down so Dad carried a box of spares to replace them with. The swather was about twelve feet wide so that's how big each swath was.

The controls were two sticks that Dad pushed forward, backward or side to side to steer the swather. There was also a control for engaging the mowing blades and for raising or lowering the sickle and rake. The swather was an awkward looking beast. The sickle and rake combination were the front part of the machine. In the middle was the engine and mechanical parts with a seat and controls for the driver up top. Underneath were two wheels, set not quite as far apart as the width of the sickle and rake mechanism. A short metal ladder welded to the side of the swather helped the driver pull himself up into the seat and there was a small metal box next to the seat where we kept a few tools.

Behind the seat, the swather had two lengths of iron that looked like I-beams. They were six or eight feet long, one welded on each side of the swather and meeting at the back of the swather in a triangular shape. On top of the triangle was a small piece of flat metal where we usually had a big rock for weight. This structure lent a little stability to the machine and ended with a small, third wheel that was there for the single purpose of allowing the swather to turn.

The rake and sickle part of the swather at the front could be raised two or three feet off the ground for moving the swather and lowered to only a few inches off the ground when it was cutting. A fun and scary part of the swather, at least for us, was that a swather is front heavy. So if you were going down a steep hayfield or road too fast, the small rear wheel came off the ground and the swather tipped forward until it was stopped with a big thump by the mowing bar in the front hitting the ground. Of course, when we first got the swather Dad neglected to mention that it might tip forward. So he thought it was very funny when we were surprised the first few times it happened when we were riding with him.

The road going over the hill to the hayfields on the West Divide Creek side of the ranch was steep and rocky. Going down that hill, the swather usually tipped forward so the rake and sickle were on the ground, and wouldn't tip back. Mom would stop and get out of the pickup where she had been following Daddy, climb up on the back of the swather on the metal plate as a counterweight while Dad kept the swather creeping slowly down the hill. Eventually, the swather tipped back so the wheel would be back on the road. Mom then jumped off the swather and went back up the hill to get the pickup where she'd left it.

Sometimes we rode with Dad when he was swathing. It was mesmerizing, watching the rake go round and round. In front of the swather was a beautiful green and purple/pink alfalfa field and behind was the orderly windrow. I thought it looked like the swather was eating the hay. If you kept an eye out, sometimes you saw field mice running through the field in front of the swather. Eventually they'd dart off to the side, into the relative protection of the still uncut part of the field or a windrow.

In years when the hay wasn't very plentiful, the windrows simply looked like a pattern mowed in the field. In a good year, the windrows could be a couple of feet deep. When hay was freshly mowed, the air smelled so sweet. It was like smelling newly cut grass, but more pungent.

Our swather and two tractors were built for functionality not comfort or for impressing the neighbors. They were all big and powerful enough to get any job on our ranch done. Our tractors didn't have even an umbrella to protect the driver from the elements. The sun was hot and unrelenting except when a late-summer high country thunderstorm would kick up. It could go from clear skies and blistering sun to a cloudburst and gully washer in a matter of minutes. Then you climbed under the piece of equipment you were on and waited it out.

The alfalfa and grass in the fields were moist when we mowed but it still created hay dust. Baling was even dustier because by then the windrows of hay had dried. Hay dust tickled your nose, got in your clothes and coated your hair.

It mixed with your sweat and with the grease from the machine, sticking to everything it touched and left an unmistakable and easily recognizable smell.

Daddy did the swathing and Grandad the baling. It was unspoken but that's the way it was and neither infringed on the others domain. Just as Dad knew when the hay and conditions were right to swath, Grandad knew when the hay was ready to bale. When he started baling in the first field Dad had swathed, putting up hay became a two-person assembly line. Dad swathed and Grandad baled a couple of days behind him until all the hay was baled.

Relatives and friends wanted to help us hay so would come out to the ranch on weekends. The help was appreciated because they worked hard and provided extra hands we didn't have. But when others helped operate our machinery, it seems like something generally went wrong. Uncle Ernie in particular liked to bale. He sincerely wanted to give Grandad a rest. One time he was on the tractor moving from one field to another. He bumped across a ditch and the baler broke down. Several other similar misfortunes happened with our equipment and helpers. Equipment in need of repair was a challenge on the ranch at any time but during haying season it was worse. When the hay was ready, it wouldn't wait on the weather or equipment problems. Also, the baler was a Massey Ferguson and the only parts available were in Meeker, 60 miles away.

If the weather held, sometimes Dad and Grandad would have to stop cutting and baling so we could do some stacking. If you left the bales in the field too long, they might get rained on or the grass would start growing up around the bales. Left long enough, the bales made a dead spot in the field where nothing grew for the next cutting.

≈

Our baler made bales that were held by two strands of twine. The weight was determined by how the tension was set on the baler. Our bales were heavy but an adult could pick up a bale to move it. It took two kids to do the same. Grandad used sisal twine when he was baling. Other people used wire to tie their bales though baling with wire was becoming less popular every year. We had quite a bit of baling wire on the place, probably left from when they used wire on our ranch. It didn't go to waste. We used baling wire to fix everything. My dad lived by the "baling wire and bubblegum" theory of fixing machinery or anything else that broke down.

They came out with plastic baling twine when I was a kid but we never used it. Grandad preferred sisal. He bought it at the Silt Co-op. When we were feeding, the baling twine was cut once to get it off the bale leaving about a five foot length which we tossed into a pile. Used twine was great for everything from tying things when we went camping to making rope ladders when we pretended to be gold miners or dreadful pirates, or braiding a makeshift halter and lead rope for catching a horse.

The bales came out of the baler on their flat (uncut) side, twine facing up. When you tilted the bale on its side, we called that the cut side. If the hay had grown tall and thick that year and the windrows were big, the baler kicked out those bales one after another. If the hay was sparse, the bales were further apart. The baler determined how tight the bales were, therefore how much hay was packed into each bale and how heavy the bales were. Our bales usually ran about thirty to the ton.

It was a tricky business getting everything with the baler set up just so. The baler is a complicated invention. Nobody but Grandad touched the baler. He knew how to string the rolls of twine together and adjust the tension on the machine so the two twines binding each bale end to end held the bale tight. A good tight bale was important to keep moisture from getting inside and molding the hay. If the tension was too tight, the bale came out the back of the baler but the twine broke when the bale hit the ground.

I think five or six rolls of twine fit in the baler at one time. One end of the twine from each roll was pulled up and over all of the rolls of twine. Grandad connected all the rolls of twine together with a series of fancy knots and intricate threading of the twine so it continued feeding through the baler with no noticeable difference in operation when one roll of twine finished and another began. Every so often, even if baling was going smoothly, Grandad pulled the metal top off the part of the baler where the twine was and checked all the rolls of twine and knots. He added more rolls of twine where needed and got them knotted into the system and ready to go.

The baler was pulled by one of our tractors so Grandad spent a lot of time getting up and down off the tractor to check the tension, add rolls of twine or move a bale that was in his way. If we were around, we liked to follow along with the baler. We'd make sure no bales were in his way when turning the tractor at the end of the windrows. It was also fun to run ahead of the baler because we would kick up the field mice hiding there like when Dad was swathing and watch them scurry away. We were supposed to kill field mice because they ate through twine and feed sacks and because they got in the house but we usually couldn't catch them. If we were following the baler and a bale broke, we'd take a pitchfork and throw the loose hay into a windrow that hadn't been baled yet.

The baler had a bale counter (mechanical) which we thought was neat because every time a bale came out, the counter automatically incremented. It was fun to run alongside when it was changing to some milestone number, say a hundred bales, for example. Grandad reset the counter at points where it made sense to him, maybe at the end of each field or each day. He kept track of the number of bales in his journal.

If it rained when Daddy was ready to swath, he had to wait for the field to dry out. Otherwise you wouldn't get the cut on the stocks of alfalfa and grasses that you wanted. A nice clean cut instead of a mangled, pulled and bent stock was easier on the equipment and helped the plants grow back better. Also, you didn't want equipment in the field when it was muddy because we didn't want any ruts made by tires and no one wanted to have to pull someone else out when they got stuck in the mud.

If it rained after the hay was cut but before it was baled, that was even bigger trouble. If the windrows weren't too thick or heavy, we'd try to give the hay a couple of days to dry out by itself. If it was a good year and the windrows were really big, or if it kept raining for several days, the windrows had to be turned over so the hay on the bottom would dry and not rot in the field. The alfalfa leaves in the hay is what provides much of the nutrition. The more the cut hay is handled, the more leaves fall off and if too much of that happens, you might as well use the hay as straw because it won't be much good as feed for the cows.

To turn the hay, we used the rake. Before we got the swather, the hay was mowed by pulling the mowing machine behind the tractor. Then the hay was put in windrows by the rake, also pulled by the tractor. After we got the swather, the rake's primary chore was not to make windrows but to turn existing windrows over to dry. This was accomplished by how the tines on the rake were positioned.

If it rained after the hay was baled but it was still out in the field, the best thing to do was to get as much of it stacked as possible before the rain soaked into the bales, rotting the hay. That's another smell I'll never forget. Hay generally smelled sweet. But if it got moldy and rotted, it smelled like something left in the back of the refrigerator.

The repetitive movement, clicking and clanking of the machinery was mesmerizing and comforting. Haying ws part of a routine that went on year in and year out. The cows and horses would be fed over the winter, they would calve or have colts in the spring and the cycle would begin again. Haying season was one of the many times I felt connected to the earth, the ranch and the legacy of my family.

≈

Where swathing and baling hay were solitary jobs, stacking it was a team effort. Many of our hayfields were on steep enough slopes that it was dangerous to pull the wagon. We had what we called the slip to pull behind the tractor for those fields. It was like a small wagon except with no wheels and no solid hitch. Instead there were two poles laid parallel to each other about the same width apart as wagon tires would be. The idea was that the poles would slide along the ground in the same direction as the tractor was pulling. Nailed across the poles were heavy planks. The slip was big enough to hold twenty or so bales of hay, depending on if you stacked them two or three high. There was also room for a couple of people doing the stacking.

The tractor pulled the slip with a heavy logging chain attached to the front corners of the slip and to the hitch of the tractor. That way, instead of chancing that the wagon tip over, taking the tractor with it, the slip slid nicely across the steep, uneven ground. Sometimes it slid away down the hill, the chain allowed that to happen, and those of us riding on the slip ended up downhill from and alongside the tractor, as if we were racing. That could be pretty exciting.

Whether we were using the wagon or slip, the tractor driver drove as close to as many bales in the hayfield as they could get. The guys and gals on the slip liked to be able to snag the bale with a hay hook and pull it onto the slip without ever stepping off. We kids did our best to make that happen and made a game of it. We'd run to a nearby bale that wasn't close enough to grab from the slip and roll it edge over edge so that the slip would go right by it. Then run to another bale, and so on. We could roll the bales faster if two of us rolled each one.

When we were stacking hay, the adults wore short horse-hide chaps. The word chaps is pronounced chaps only in the east. In the west, we pronounce it, correctly I might add, shaps. These chaps were made of soft, sturdy, gray colored leather and were only used for moving hay. They buckled loosely around the waist over the belt. The front of the chaps was a solid piece of leather going down each leg to below the knee and wrapping part way around the leg on each side. The back of the leg wasn't covered but had two straps of leather that pulled the chaps loosely around the leg. Each strap was sewn on one side of the chap and hooked with a metal pinch-hook into a metal ring on the other side.

Heavy but pliable leather work gloves were worn for almost all ranch chores. Usually I didn't like to wear gloves but they were a must when we were doing things with the sharp, stickery hay. Work gloves needed to fit your hand "like a glove", so when buying new gloves, you didn't just take any pair off the shelf. Like our boots and hats, gloves were costly and we would have them for a long time if we took care of them. So we tried on gloves before buying a pair. Dad and Grandad had a favorite brand that they bought, usually at the Silt Co-op.

We kids either rolled bales or used the twine to move bales around. The adults used hay hooks. Hay hooks are just what they sound like. The handle was made of wood about as wide as the grip of an adult man. The hook was big, sharp and scary looking but also surprisingly balanced and, with a little practice, easy to use. Hay hooks always reminded me of Captain Hook in Peter Pan. A big, strong person could hold a hay hook in each hand and with a flick of the wrist, bury the hook up to its hilt in the hay in the middle of each end of the bale. You couldn't carry a bale far that way. But if you put your knee into the bale, you could grab a bale, heft it up and put it on a wagon or a stack of bales. Sometimes we each took one hay hook, stuck them in on each end of the bale and then two of us could carry it from one place to another although it was heavy and awkward. More often, we snagged one end of a bale and drug it.

More often than not, I grabbed the twine. It could take quite a bit of abuse but you didn't want to get too enthusiastic because you could pull one or both of the twines off the bale, or break one. Either way, the bale would mini-explode and instead of one tight, compact bale of hay that was easily managed, you had a pile of dried stems and leaves that you had to move with a pitchfork, a scoop shovel, or by picking up as much as you could in your arms.

After the wagon or slip was full of hay, everybody, including those of us that had been running along beside, climbed up on the hay and caught a break and a ride to the haystack for a drink of cold water.

At dinner time, everybody headed for either our house or Grandma and Grandad's. Even though they'd been helping in the hayfields all morning, Mom and Grandma would have a full meat and potatoes dinner on the table. Often we had a beef roast and there was always cake or cobbler for dessert. Haying crews eat hearty. Not only was it time for hard workers to eat, it also let everybody take a short rest before hitting it hard again that afternoon. Haying was hot, dusty and dry work. Spending a little time in the cool house in the middle of the day was a welcome break.

The last few years that we were on the ranch, there were lots of changes in farm machinery. Except for the swather, we never bought any of it. All of this machinery was specialized to one task. What we had was more general use, the same machinery could be used for many different jobs. Daddy said those huge tractors and other farm machinery were way too pricey and too much power for the jobs to be done. It was one of those things he called "keeping up with the Joneses." And of course we didn't have a big enough operation or the money for anything extra, including expensive farm equipment. Some ranches had a baler that had its own motor and driver's seat so you didn't have to pull it with a tractor like you did ours. Our baler worked just fine and we didn't need an expensive new baler. Besides, Dad said it would be just one more engine to mess with.

Another new piece of farm machinery on the market was an automatic stacker. It picked up the bales out of the field, had a short conveyor belt to move the bales onto a platform on the stacker, and stacked mini-haystacks about ten bales high and five or six bales wide, maybe the same deep. When it was full, you drove the stacker to the stack yard and released the mini stack, standing it on end and leaning it against the previous stacker load. It made stacking hay a one person job but there was lots of space between each stacker load for moisture to get between the bales. The first mini-stack was propped up with poles and all the mini-stacks tended to lean slightly against the previous one. So hay stacks put up with the stacker were more prone to falling down. I never saw a haystack Dad built fall down. Also when you stacked hay with the stacker, the haystack was only as tall as the stacker wagon so you needed a much bigger stack yard than when you were stacking by hand.

There were also balers that made two kinds of very large bales that were quite popular with the new generation of ranchers. One made a rectangular bale shaped much like our bales but weighing about half a ton each. They stacked nicely but besides the baler, you needed a heavy duty tractor with a forklift on the front to move, stack and feed the hay. The other made big round bales about the same size. Again, it was a different baler and a heavy duty tractor. The round bales needed huge stack yards because you could only stack them two or three bales high. And there was lots of space between those round bales for moisture to get into the hay. Both of these big bales of hay meant that you had to have at least two people to feed a bunch of cows.

Using any of those three methods of stacking, more hay was wasted, lost to rot and mold. A good stacker, like my Dad, could build a tall haystack where the bales were so tight together that the only hay affected by moisture was on the very edges of the bales on the outside and top of the stack. This meant less mold, so less waste.

≈

Building a haystack by hand was already mostly a lost art when I was a kid. Anybody could stack bales of hay, I suppose, but Daddy was a true, old fashioned hay stacker. His buddy, Luther Fuller was a good stacker so he was happy if Luther visited from Denver during haying season. Our hay stacks were tall, not very big around and absolutely water tight. Our fairly small haystacks (they went up, not out) required a small stack yard. Since much of the ranch was hillside, flat space was at a premium and we used all of it, except for the stack yards and our houses, for hayfields and pastures. We had four or five stack yards on the place. When feeding the cows over the winter, rather than hauling the hay to the cattle, we moved the cattle to the hay.

From experience, Dad knew the optimum size for a single haystack. Getting the bottom tier right was the key to the whole stack. He took a lot of time on that first tier. Then, they made the hay stack go up magically, each layer tying into the prior one.

The bottom layer, or tier, of the haystack stood on the cut sides. The bales were placed end to end and making corners until you had a square of single file bales. When setting the bales in place, Dad butted each bale securely up against the previous bale so there was as little space as possible between them. The rest of the bales were also set in cut side up but they didn't follow the outer ring, they were placed in rows within the outer ring. If everything went as planned and the tier was good and tight with minimum space between all the bales, getting the last bale in place could take a little cussing and stamping on it.

For all the other tiers, bales were stacked on the flat side, cross-cut style, with the cut sides touching the other bales in that tier. Dad tied in the corners of each tier and by the time he was done, even if the haystack was 18 or 20 tiers high, the top tier was exactly the same size as the first. Dad's haystacks never fell down and they didn't even bulge as the winter wore on and hay was taken from the stack to feed.

When the haystack was too tall to lift, shove or pull the bales up on it, we had a hay elevator that solved the problem nicely. It had two sturdy rails set about as wide as a bale of hay and a conveyor belt with cast iron links and sharp tines. The tines caught in the bottom of the bale and kept it from falling off the elevator as it was hauled upward. The whole thing was run by a gasoline motor attached to the elevator which we started by pulling a rope. We hauled the elevator from haystack to haystack on the wagon or the slip. It was heavy and awkward and took two people to move it. We girls loved to help on top of the stack and as each bale tipped over the top, we moved it out of the way for the next bale. If the haystack was too tall to clamber up, we had to perch on the elevator and ride it up and down which was a bit scary. How fast the bales came up the haystack depended entirely on who was putting them on at the bottom of the stack. If it was Mom or Grandad, they spaced them nicely. If it was Uncle Steve or Uncle Ernie, sometimes they put them on one right after the other just to make whoever was on top of the stack holler.

During haying season, the gnats were unbearable. Besides avoiding sunburn, the gnats were another reason we always wore long sleeved shirts. But still the almost invisible little buggers got in your nose and ears, and buzzed around your eyes. We called them no-see-ums! They didn't really bite or sting like a mosquito or a bee and you didn't swell up from their bites but they sure were annoying.

When we were haying, we took the old Clorox jugs out of the freezer and filled them on up with water. As the ice melted we had cold water all day long. We put the water jug in the shade of the stack as the haystack went up and moved it as the day wore on to make sure it stayed in the shade. We didn't waste water and the haying crew all took a drink break at the same time. Nothing tastes better than a swig of that cold spring water from the jug while taking a break, sitting in the shade of the haystack with the rest of Grandad and Daddy's "petticoat crew."

A lot of sounds and smells bring back memories of the ranch, none more so than during haying season. The smell of sisal twine or gunnysacks in the hot sun, mixed with freshly cut hay is very nice. Even the smell of the last of the hay in the spring that was getting a bit moldy was pungent but not unpleasant. No matter what equipment we had and how many friends and relatives came to help, haying was hard work. Getting the job done was an example of the strong work ethic, willpower and determination running a cattle ranch requires. I was proud to be considered part of the crew.

In winter, deer and elk came into our hayfields to feed. Besides digging through the snow and grazing, they learned that haystacks were an easier way to get a full belly than foraging in the cedars. So we put up deer fence around each haystack. It was about eight or ten feet tall and made of one by fours wired together about 3 or 4 inches apart so the fence was flexible. As each stack was depleted during the winter feeding, each length of deer fence was rolled up and stowed in a pile. Putting up the deer fence meant unrolling what you needed, wiring two or more lengths of deer fence together and leaning it against the haystack. If the deer fence was broken, it was easily fixed by putting in a new board or wiring it back together. Mom used the broken boards for firewood. I think the Fish and Game Department or Department of Wildlife supplied deer fence to any rancher who made the request.

≈

Down through the barnyard at the lower place, there was a wooden bridge across the creek. As was common on the ranch, wherever there was a fairly steady supply of water, there were huge cottonwood trees. Through the cottonwoods, the road went by a fenced-in pen that was maybe an acre in size. This was what we called Jimmy's Pen where Daddy kept our big stud horse, Star Bar Jim. Before that, Grandma Arthur had a garden there. The summer Aunt Ruthie and Mom were pregnant with Wes and me, they helped Grandma in the garden. It was a huge garden and lots of back-breaking work out in the hot sun.

Hamilton Arthur and his family had a garden there as well when they owned the place. Uncle Ham's daughter, Catherine, kept strictly to a planting schedule which she had developed.

Planting Times   (Catherine Arthur, 1930s)

> Peas: April 1st to July 1st
> Beans: May 1st to June 25th (Kentucky wonder)
> Corn: May 1st to June 15th
> Turnip: April 1st to July 15th or little later
> Carrots: May 1st
> Beets: May 2st to July 1st
> Parsnips: May 1st
> Salsify: May 1st
> Cabbage: hot bed – in garden April 1st
> Tomatoes: June 1st

Green peppers: June 1st
Watermelon: May 1st
Cantaloupe: May 1st
Cucumber: May 1st
Squash: May 1st
Lettuce: May 1st to July 15th
Radish: May 1st to August 1st
Green onions: April 1st
Onion seed: May 1st
Celery: April 1st in hot bed
Cauliflower: April 1st in hot bed
Chard: May 2st to August
Spinach: May 1st (one planting)

I had to look up "salsify", pronounced "salsifee". It is sometimes called oyster plant and has a root much like a parsnip.

Beyond Jimmy's pen, the road went by a row of chokecherry trees, then turned 90 degrees right into some hayfields. Across the fence from those hayfields, you were in a pasture belonging to our neighbor, Mr. Hall. Somewhere in that pasture was the site of the old town of Raven which had its own post office and school in the 1890s and early 1900s.

The road went through another hayfield and headed up a steep, rocky hill. In a couple of spots it was narrow with the sagebrush and cedar hillside going straight up on one side and a nasty little drop off down towards Hall's hayfields on the other. The road sidled around and up the hill, then topped out on the ridge and dropped down through a nice stand of cedars and pinons to the hayfields. When we talked about these two big hayfields, we said we were "going over the hill." The stack yard was in the middle of the field near the lower ditch. At the bottom of the hayfields, the ditch continued on around the hill and eventually ended, letting any remaining water spread out on the hillside.

Below the hayfields was an excellent spring that hadn't been developed. The water was cool and delicious. A deer trail went along the spring. Above the trail, there was a steep rocky hill. We loved to scramble up the hill and look for flint chips, arrowheads and beads. There must have been a Ute camp there because every spring, more chips and parts of arrowheads, spearheads and fleshing knives washed up. There were several old Ute camps on and around the ranch where we looked for arrowheads. It was one of our favorite pastimes. Dad had lots of broken arrowheads and a dozen or more perfect ones he found over the years walking and riding horseback on the ranch and the BLM and National Forest in the high country above the place.

When the ranch was sold, thirty acres below the hayfields and including the spring were kept. Grandma and Grandad built a house above the West Divide Creek road, put in a cistern and used the spring for their water. Later, Mom and Dad also built a house on that property farther up the hill and drilled a well for water.

From the hayfields, the whole valley opened up and it was a great view. You could see all the way to the Grand Hogbacks and Flat Tops on the north. To the west there were lots of ranches, farms, fields and pastures and several drainages. First there was West Divide Creek, then Dry Hollow, then Mamm Creek. Farther to the west was

Mamm Mountain and the Bookcliffs (Roan Plateau) to the northwest, past Rifle. Uncle Bob Mountain and Buzzard Pass were to the south. it was spectacular.

Horse Sense   11

Whereas the land, hay and cows on the ranch belonged to Grandad Arthur, the horses were ours. Besides hunting season when Dad was a guide and outfitter and took people hunting, selling a couple of colts every year was our only source of income that Mom didn't have to ask from Grandad. Since the business of the ranch was raising cattle and the hay to feed them, our horses were important. We rode the ranch to check fence lines and see how the hay crop was coming along. We rode to gather and move the cows, and during hunting season. And we rode for fun.

We usually had most of the horses in the pasture next to our house, down on the creek bottom, or out in the yard, grazing on whatever was sweet, tender and green. During the summer, there was enough grass and pasture that we didn't have to feed. But if we were working cows, the horses we used earned a flake of hay and some grain at the end of the day.

Besides eating what they were supposed to, our horses loved flowers, especially petunias, marigolds and hollyhocks from Mom's flower beds. They also liked lilac blossoms, all roses and the pink flowers that thistles had in the spring. Mom tried several times to grow roses and lilacs in our front yard. But about the time the bushes were growing and thriving, they were also just tall enough to reach the belly of a horse. Besides eating the leaves and blooms, our horses loved to scratch their bellies on Mom's lilac and rose bushes and generally killed the bushes, or at least stunted their growth. What the horses didn't eat, the deer got. Made my mom nuts.

Many of our horses were green-broke. Our green-broke horses were often three or four year olds that you could get bridled and saddled and they would tolerate a rider without turning it into a rodeo. Or at least with a minimum of bucking and kicking. They had little to no training, didn't neck rein much, and didn't like the cinch on the saddle, the saddle blanket or saddle on its back, the bit in its mouth or the bridle headstall over its ears. They especially didn't like the idea of a rider. These were the horses Dad usually rode to do ranch work because all the nice, gentle, saddle broke horses that neck reined and worked with the rider were being ridden by our ever present town company that came out to the ranch to help. Tammi and I weren't very old when Daddy decided we were pretty good hands so we got the best horses.

Our good horses included Barfly, Red Wing, Biscuit, Rambler and Diamond. Diamond was more brown than sorrel and had a diamond shape right in the middle of his forehead. He was Uncle Ernie's favorite. Diamond was an old horse and had been on the ranch for a long time. The younger horses were Little Joe (named after Dad's friend, Joe Morris), Cricket, Thunder, Choco and Muffin. Muffin, you might guess from the name, was Biscuit's foal. Among others, we also had Little Red, Barbie, Dandy, Vicky and San Can. It was common for the horses on our ranch to live well into their twenties.

Thunder was one of Red Wing's colts. I remember well the night he was born. It was a nasty, cold and wet night. The rain poured down and the thunder and lightning boomed and cracked all over the place. Red Wing picked her spot which happened to be in our yard, up the hill from the house and across the path going to the outhouse. It was in the trees but only a few steps from the corner of the living room. Mom let us stay up way past our bedtime because a new colt on the place was always a big deal. My folks checked on Red from time to time, going out in the rain with a flashlight. We watched from the living room window. The minute the colt was born, we named him Thunder.

We always called our young horses colts. In proper terms, baby horses are called foals. A male is a colt and a female is a filly. On the ranch, we pretty much just called them all colts. The adult horses on the ranch, except for our one stud, were all mares or geldings. You didn't want to be riding either a stud or a mare if any of the mares were in heat. They got single minded and cranky and it could be dangerous for the rider. Some geldings acted goofy around mares in heat too. Dad called them proud cut and said they'd either been gelded incorrectly or were too old when they were gelded.

I was so young the first time I was put on a horse that I don't remember it at all. When we were still babies and toddlers, we rode in the saddle in front of the adults. We also rode bareback, holding onto the horse's mane with both hands while someone led the horse around the pasture. There are pictures of four or five of us toddler cousins sitting on one horse and having a great time. We were going for a ride.

We had several kid's horses over the years, starting with Tony, Old Paint and then Vicky. We asked for a pony several times because that seemed to be what town kids always wanted. Dad said he wouldn't have a pony on the place because they were mean, hard headed and obstinate and he didn't want us around one because we might get hurt. So we had to ask for help until we were big enough or until we figured out how to catch our regular big horse and get on.

I'm not sure what defined what was a kid's horse but to me it meant that they were old and gentle. They didn't belong to any particular kid but were shared by all. Our horses tended to be one of the biggest, if not necessarily the tallest, horses on the ranch. Besides being too old to work on the ranch, I'm sure they were picked because they were the least likely to be skittish, run away with us or run right over us if we were on the ground. Even with the best of intentions on the part of the horse, we were often stepped on, mainly because we weren't paying attention when the horse decided to move around.

All the kid's horses we had through the years were pretty easy to catch and let us throw the lead rope up and over their neck so we could tie it. Then we led the horse back to the house to get help putting the bridle on and getting a boost up. At that age, and with minimal adult supervision, we generally rode bareback. Tony had such a long, wide back that we could easily ride double. Inevitably, whoever was riding got off for some reason. If no one was around to give us a boost up, we got creative finding things to stand on. If we could get the horse close enough, a big rock, tree stump, stack of firewood, pile of lumber, corral fence, or overturned bucket worked nicely. When we were a little bigger and stronger, sometimes we could get Tony to lower his head. Then we wrapped our arms around his neck and scramble up that way.

As we got older, at some point we must have demonstrated that we could be trusted around our horse. With that trust came more freedom. As long as Mom knew what we were up to, we could go riding father away from the house. We got good about double teaming old Tony with the bridle. One of us climbed up on something and held the headstall up. If I was holding the headstall, as soon as Tammi got the bit in Tony's mouth, I pulled the top of the bridle over his ears. Voila!

Sometimes we rode with just the halter and lead rope looped over Paint's neck as reins. More often than not, we didn't use a halter at all. We only had a few halters on the place and it was too much trouble to make sure that we got the halter returned to the shed each and every time we wanted to use one. So we fashioned baling twine together with knots to make a rudimentary hackamore and reins.

The stud horse we had was papered as a registered quarter horse. His official name was Star Bar Jim but we called him Jimmy. We got him from Joe Morris. Joe had started out as one of Dad's rich Texas hunters and became a family friend for many years. Jimmy was a big, tall, dark colored horse. I think he was a bay but he may have been a dark sorrel. We were told to stay away from him because he was very big, high spirited, and a little nuts, especially when there were mares anywhere around. Jimmy's pen was across the creek at Grandma and Grandad's house where Grandma's vegetable garden used to be.

East Divide Creek ran right down through the middle of the ranch. As we did in several pastures that were near the creek, we built a nifty little livestock watering system in Jimmy's pen. In one side of the pasture, a portion of the fence was removed and a V-shaped fence was built from the pasture fence down the bank and out into the creek. Simple solution.

While still a fairly young horse, Jimmy suddenly died of a heart attack. Grandad fed him a full three pound coffee can of grain twice a day along with his hay. Earlier that year we had had a vet out to look at a sick cow and he went to look at Jimmy. Even then, the vet told Grandad that Jimmy was gaining too much weight and not getting enough exercise.

At some point shortly after Jimmy died, Dad won another stud horse in a poker game. This was good news because we liked to have colts every year. He won this horse from Joe Morris too. Joe and Dad loved to play poker even though Joe was well off and Dad really had nothing much to bet with. It's a good thing Dad was a good poker player.

So one day, we all got in the pickup and headed to Ft. Collins to pick up the new stud horse. Dad had seen the horse, or at least a picture of him, I don't know which. The only thing the rest of the family knew about him was that he was papered and that he was a paint, not a pinto, which I had always thought was the same thing. His short name was San Moteado. When Mom and we girls saw the horse for the first time, we saw that he wasn't very big and the poor thing had the ugliest head of any horse we had ever seen. I love horses but let me tell you, this one was definitely ugly. But San Moteado threw the most beautiful foals. No matter what the mare looked like, the colt was a paint and was beautiful in conformation and looks. Vicky was a black horse, so her colts were black and white paints. Sorrel mares had red and white paints. One of the colts that Tammi fell in love with had a perfectly shaped red heart on its side.

We were partial to sorrel horses on the ranch. They had beautiful reddish brown coats, some variety of white blaze down their noses, and white stockings. Some of our horses had wide blazes, some had narrow blazes and some had a white star shape or some other white spot on their forehead. Some had four white stockings, some less than that. Some had shorter stockings up to their fetlocks, others had stockings all the way to their knees. Some had stockings that were evenly matched, some had both short and tall stockings that we thought were funny.

All of our horses were quarter horses, or mostly quarter horse. They weren't real big or tall but very sturdy and dependable for doing ranch work. They also were good at keeping their footing on steep, rocky hillsides. Our horses were mountain horses with great stamina and heart. Even at the end of a long, tiring day, I always knew my horse would get me home, safe and sound. They had the endurance and personality to work hard all day long and they were very smart. Many times when I was unsure about a tricky spot such as a steep hillside or a boggy area, I let my horse have her head and pick her own route and footing.

≈

We used both bridles and hackamores. There are many kinds of bits used in bridles, some more harsh (in my opinion) than others. We only had one kind of bit on the ranch, a solid bit with the least severe curve in any bit that was available. A hackamore has no bit at all. There is a special type of knot at the bottom of the headstall under the horse's chin where the reins are attached. Sometimes called a bosal hackamore, we just called the knot under the horse's chin the bosal and Dad tried to show us how to tie it several times but we never quite got it right.

If a horse neck reined, it didn't matter if you used a bridle or a hackamore, Either way, it's never okay to jerk on a horse's head and mouth. With a bridle, in a short amount of time you can tear up the inside of their mouth and their tongue. Not only is it painful for the horse, but if it goes on for long periods of time, the horse will get hard-mouthed. The scar tissue builds up, the horse remembers how he's been treated and in the future, it doesn't matter what kind of bit you use, you'll get no response from the horse except rebellion and belligerence. A bridle and bit are certainly appropriate for some horses and circumstances. It's just that you have to take care whenever there is metal in a horse's mouth and you have control of the reins. It is far too easy to get mad or careless and jerk on his mouth.

When we were riding, we were always mindful of making sure the two reins were even and not pulled tight against the horse's mouth. Still, I don't know how many times I heard my dad holler at us "give that horse some slack" or "stop pulling on that horse's head."

When using a hackamore, all commands to the horse are done by pressure from your knees and from the rein on their neck. Whether using a bridle or a hackamore, a well trained horse knows to turn left if you lay the rein against his neck on the right side and press your right knee into his side. Same concept for turning right. We had horses that we always rode with a hackamore and they never had, or needed, a bit in their mouth.

Some people would argue that you had more control with a bridle and bit. I tend to believe that if the horse is well trained and the horse and rider know each other well enough, a mutual trust and respect grows and control isn't even an issue. Sure, kids and horses can both get hard headed at times and with some horses it was a constant power struggle, but you just worked it out. I feel the same way about spurs as I do about severe or harsh bits on bridles. We had spurs but I never wore them unless I was on an extremely spoiled horse. Kicking the heel of your boot against their gut was usually enough to get the horse's attention when you needed to get going. If that seems like an oversimplification and rosy picture of life with horses, it is. Don't be fooled. I've spent plenty of time fighting with my horse instead of working with her to get the job done. I can still feel the aggravation of matching wits with a stubborn horse and ending up in tears.

We kept the tack to a minimum, using a light saddle pad and a western saddle with a single cinch that went around the horse's belly. The rigging was for functionality more than appearance though we did take pride in how our horses and tack looked and how we cared for them. The saddle pad's purpose was to keep the motion of the rider in the saddle from rubbing a saddle sore on the horse's back. So it's important that the horse's hair is lying flat and that the saddle pad is centered on the horse's back behind the withers. The saddle is centered on top of the pad and then it's time to tighten the cinch.

The cinch has to be tight enough to hold the saddle on but not too tight to rub a sore on the horse's side or belly. Actually, I've never seen anyone get a cinch too tight. I'm sure it's possible with a strong man. But no chance of a kid getting the cinch too tight. I have seen the opposite. When you're saddling a horse and tightening the cinch, almost every horse will blow himself as full of air as possible. After he walks around for a few minutes, he blows all the extra air out and now the cinch is way too loose again. A smart rider will tighten down the cinch as much as she can, lead the horse around for a bit, then tighten the cinch again before ever setting foot in the stirrup. If the cinch isn't tight when you step into the saddle, both saddle and rider slip sideways. The best thing to do in that case is to step down and basically start over. This is a clumsy, awkward and embarrassing maneuver so best to be avoided in the first place.

Any length of leather left hanging down after the cinch is tight is tucked through a ring or slit in the leather of the saddle skirt. You don't want anything hanging down from the saddle that might distract the horse or get tangled. There was lots of oak brush, sage brush and various other kinds of bushes in our country. Going riding on the ranch inevitably meant riding through brush that would snag any loose clothing or tack it could reach.

Length of stirrups can be adjusted depending on the height of the rider. The correct length is so that when standing in the stirrups, there's "enough" space between your behind and the saddle seat. Older saddles had the stirrups laced on with strips of leather. Those took some time to adjust because you had to unlace and re-lace. Our newer saddles had a flat buckle mechanism that made changing stirrup lengths quick and easy.

One time our cousin Bobby got a kid's saddle. It had a kid-sized seat, cantle, saddle horn and stirrups. It was beautiful and of course we wanted one too. Of course we couldn't afford one. But Dad's explanation was that we didn't need one. If the stirrups on a regular saddle couldn't be shortened enough for us, we'd have to ride bareback until we grew a little more. Long before we were able to actually get the saddle up on the horse, we were half carrying, half dragging our saddles out of the shed for Mom or Dad to saddle our horses for us. But we sure did like Bobby's neat new kid saddle.

Anything you do with a ranch horse is from the left side of the horse. You stand to the left when putting on the bridle, the saddle pad and saddle, and when you tighten the cinch. You do, of course, walk around to the right side to check the saddle to make sure that nothing is twisted or tucked under the fender. You also mount and dismount on the left.

You may see horses out in the pasture wearing a halter. Not on our ranch. We never left a halter on a horse when we turned them out. Dad said that a horse could get the halter hung up on a fence post or tree branch too easily. When attaching a lead rope to a halter, we used a bowline knot. We practiced tying bowlines over and over until Dad was satisfied with our results. The bowline would hold fast but you could also get the knot undone in a hurry if you needed to. Newer lead ropes had a snap hook on the end to hook onto the halter. Mom and Dad got a fancy leather lead rope which we used when we were showing horses at the Fair. Later, someone gave me a twisted green and white halter and matching lead rope made of nylon for Christmas or my birthday. I thought it was the best present ever.

Sometimes we had spoiled horses on the place. I suspect they were either given to Dad or he bought them cheap because the previous owner got frustrated when they couldn't get the horse to do anything. The spoiled horses we had showed a variety of bad habits and I ended up riding them all, more than once. Horses can be very creative when they're being ornery. I suppose that a spoiled horse can be retrained, given enough time and patience, but bad habits are hard to break.

One of our horses threw her head so you had to constantly adjust the reins. She pulled them through your hands, you shortened them up, and that process got real old real fast. With her, we used a breast collar added to the front of the saddle. A leather strap covered with sheepskin was buckled to the front of the saddle on each side and went across the horse's chest. A narrow leather strap went from the center of the breast collar, between the horse's front legs and attached to the cinch. Another narrow leather strap called a tie down was attached to the bottom of the headstall and to the breast collar, effectively keeping the horse from throwing her head

Except for Dad, none of us had a saddle that we called our own although we all did have our favorite that we would choose if we had the chance. Dad had a custom made saddle that he had ordered from a saddle maker in Texas using his own specifications. It had a deep seat with a high cantle and tall, narrow saddle horn. The leather was dark brown and we girls spent a fair amount of time with the saddle soap and rags, working on his saddle. No one rode that saddle except Daddy and on the ranch it was the only saddle he ever used.

We always had horses to ride and play with and knew which horses we could be around and which ones to stay away from. And we knew that if we got around a young, unbroken, spoiled or otherwise cantankerous animal, we needed to be more scared of Dad than we were of the horse.

≈

When I was nine or ten years old, Tammi and I each got a horse that we could call our own. My colt was a funny looking little bay filly named Cricket. Dad had loaned one of our ranch quarter horses, a light sorrel named Barfly, to Aunt Nancy's sister, Laurie. Barfly was one of our best ranch horses. Laurie used Barfly for barrel racing and pole bending at rodeos and gymkhanas. Apparently no one realized that the horse was pregnant until she started making bag a few days before the birth. Thus came Cricket on Mother's Day, May 15. Because of the hard use Barfly had had while she was pregnant, Cricket was never a very big horse and her conformation wasn't quite right. Some years later, Daddy figured out that somehow Cricket had had her back broken when she was born or shortly after, before we got her and Barfly back on the ranch. But that didn't keep her from being a great little horse for me to grow up with.

Having my own horse was a big responsibility and at first I felt a little resentment because taking care of Cricket was my number one job and it was a full time job. But after awhile I liked having Cricket underfoot all the time and she was a pet, almost like a big puppy. We soon became best friends. I spent my time teaching Cricket to lead, brushing her and messing with her feet so she got used to having me around. Before long, I looped the lead rope over her neck and she followed me everywhere. Several times she followed me up on the front porch and if Mom would have let us, Cricket would have gone right on in the house.

While Cricket was a yearling and still too small to ride, I took horsemanship in 4H and she was my project. Mr. Norell over on Dry Hollow was the leader. Mom hauled Cricket to my horsemanship meetings in the back of our pickup. Our first module was all about learning the parts of a horse. We had detailed drawings in our project workbook but our leader also quizzed us while we were with our horses. We learned about tack, and then about the parts of the foot and how to take care of our horse's feet. All of the 4H members in my club were ranch and farm kids so none of this was new to us.

Our summer 4H meetings were spent leading our horses, getting them to walk and stand to their best advantage. It was all about getting ready for the various classes in which we would compete at the Fair. At the Fair, we would be judged on several things including the horse's conformation, movement and presentation. Training and hard work over the summer was key and the judge could tell how much time you spent with your horse by how the 4H member and her horse interacted. The judge also watched how the horse acted around the other horses and youngsters.

Getting ready for Fair, we practiced over and over leading our young horses to a smooth but quick stop, teaching them to set their feet firmly on the ground and squared up under their body. This was the best way to show a horse's conformation when the judge looked at the horse's chest, shoulders, back and hips. With lots of practice, Cricket set up her feet automatically every time she stopped, front feet even under the chest, back feet nice and straight behind them. I had to watch her though because Cricket had a bad habit of cocking her right rear leg so her foot was tilted, leaning on the front of the hoof rather than sitting it squarely on the ground.

That first year I showed Cricket, I was a basket case. The project book was easy for me because I was good at doing reports and such. But that was only one part of the consideration to see whether you got a blue, red or white ribbon. My folks went all out. I had brand new western polyester pants, not blue jeans, and a fancy long sleeved western shirt. My hair had never been braided so neatly. My hat was clean, my boots polished to a high shine.

The big parking lot at the Fairgrounds in Rifle was full of pickups and horse trailers. My folks were so proud of us. It was exciting buzzing around, getting our horses ready and watching all the other kids do the same thing. We brushed their coats to a beautiful shine and cleaned their feet over and over again until their hooves glistened in the sun. We made sure their manes, tails, forelocks and fetlocks were clean and brushed out. We checked and rechecked our tack, hats, hair and boots. When my class was finally called, it was exciting but nerve wracking as we all entered the arena.

When Cricket was big enough for me to ride, Daddy broke her and me at the same time. She still wasn't big enough to stand the weight of an adult so with me aboard and him on the ground, he taught Cricket how to neck rein, change leads and mind what I wanted her to do. Mostly. And he taught me how to teach a horse to do those things. Even though my horse and I were already best friends, this started a whole new love-hate, testing of the wills relationship between us.

I had already been playing with Cricket for weeks getting ready to actually break her. First I got her used to the saddle blanket a little at a time until I could throw it up on her back without making her spook. Since we started when Cricket was so young and I was going to spend so much time working with her, it made sense to break her to a hackamore. That was fine by me because I've never been fond of using a bridle and bit if you don't need to. The hackamore was no problem when I first put it on her because it wasn't that different from the halter and lead rope she was used to.

We had a couple of horses on the place that hated having their ears messed with so it was a chore getting the headstall of the bridle up and over their ears. Cricket wasn't like that. I had played with her so much that she liked having her ears scratched and tickled. Sometimes when she wanted her head rubbed, she pushed so hard with her head against my hand or shoulder that she almost knocked me over.

The saddle was next. Even though I wasn't very big, neither was Cricket. So I could lift the saddle up onto her back without dragging it up there. The first several times, I made sure both stirrups and cinch were stacked neatly in the seat of the saddle so as little as possible was hanging off the saddle to make noise or flap around and spook Cricket. Then I slowly and carefully took the stirrups down, leaving the cinch pulled up on top of the saddle.

Cricket spent a lot of time standing around with the saddle on her back while I brushed her and played with her feet. Then I started fastening the cinch enough so I could lead her around without the saddle falling off or sliding too far to one side or the other. Each day I tightened the cinch a little more until one day she was saddled, ready to ride, and didn't even know it. During those weeks I spent a lot of time jumping up over her bare back and just laying there.

Our corral was small and round with high pole fences. Most of our practicing had been around the place during the course of our days rather than in the corral. But Cricket saw no problem going in the corral. Dad held her as I put my foot in the stirrup and stepped up. Still no problem. Working up to me actually climbing aboard had been a good idea. We spent time over several days with Daddy leading Cricket around the corral with me aboard. Then I rode her around the corral with Dad giving her a pat, actually more like a smack than a pat, on the rump for encouragement from time to time. We rode as close to the fence as possible. In fact, my jeans pant leg or the toe of my boot often rubbed against the corral rails.

Next, I spent hours over several days alone with my horse, riding Cricket around the corral at a walk. Around and around, pressing with my knees and laying the reins on her neck, getting her used to neck reining. I also trotted her around in circles, and loped once in awhile, changing directions when I thought we were both about to get dizzy. This is where Dad really got to work. We spent much of the rest of the summer working together afternoons and evenings. Daddy stood in the center of the corral, watching Cricket and me work. We walked, trotted or loped around at a pretty good clip, changing directions every now and then and I thought we were doing well with the neck reining. I wasn't pulling on Cricket's head and she was responding, mostly, to my neck reining clues with reins and knees.

When Dad didn't think Cricket was turning fast enough, he stepped out in front of her, waved his arms and yelled "ha!" The first few times he did it, his little maneuver surprised me and I almost lost my seat. It surprised Cricket too. She perked up her ears, got wide-eyed and did a little skid-stop-turn all in one motion. After that, we got better at it and Cricket and I started working together to anticipate when Dad was going to decide that we should change directions. Eventually, Dad sat up on the top rail of the corral and told me when to change. Cricket and I got to where we could swap ends on demand, changing leads in a fairly smooth fashion. All in all, even given many moments of frustration and with patience wearing thin, Cricket was a nice little riding horse for me.

When I was a third year horsemanship member in 4H, Cricket and I moved from leading to riding. Showing at the Fair included riding around the rodeo arena with the other horses and riders in your class. The judge stood in the center of the arena and called out when he or she wanted us to change gaits: trot, walk, trot, lope and so on. They also watched how well we worked with our horse to change leads.

A correct lead means that the horse's inside leg will reach farther forward than his outside leg. If the horse is going to the left, they should be in a left lead, going to the right in a right lead. When a horse is in the correct lead, it helps with their balance so they're not constantly shifting weight. The horse takes clues from the rider when to change leads in one smooth motion, especially when they make a quick change of directions. Examples of making quick changes are in the pole bending competition at a rodeo or when a good cutting horse moves to separate one calf from the rest of the herd.

One of my favorite events was western pleasure which is basically like an obstacle course for horses. Among other things, you demonstrated that your horse was trained by backing between two logs lying on the ground. This is not trivial because not all horses are good at or comfortable with moving straight backward. There was a mail box you had to open, on horseback, put an envelope in, close the mail box and put up the flag. There was a wooden bridge to walk up and over without the horse spooking or balking.

The hardest trick for most of us was the wooden gate. Without dismounting, the rider had to get close enough to the gate to unlatch it, open the gate, ride through and re-latch it. When you and your horse got good at it, you could do all of that without ever letting go of the gate.

More Horse Sense   12

Our summers were full with all of our 4H projects, helping our folks on the ranch and lots of camping and fishing in the high country. Tammi and I also spent parts of several summers helping Bill and Carol Porter, the pool riders at East Divide Cow Camp. Usually we rode their horses but one time we took Cricket to cow camp for me to ride. As usual, Cricket was in the back of the pickup. With a horse aboard, Dad took it pretty easy going up the road into the high country. Just above the Moore place, our upper pasture, the road goes up a very steep, rocky hill. About half way up, there's a bend in the road. We were making our way around that corner when two teenagers on dirt bikes came screaming down the road, cutting the corner so they were on the same side of the road as we were and directly in our path.

It happened in a split second, so fast it was over before I even knew we had hit one of the kids on the dirt bikes.

The impact threw Cricket to her knees but she got right up and wasn't hurt. My parents jumped out and told us to stay in the pickup. Eventually, they let us get out. The girl and the bike were both completely under the pickup and, of course, her brother was very upset. Somehow, Mom and Dad got her out from under the pickup. They didn't want to move her too much until they figured out how bad it was. She was all skinned up and the kick stand had dug into her leg. There was lots of blood. Later, we learned besides all the scrapes, cuts and bruises, she had a broken leg.

The girl went into shock and of course we didn't have any blankets, water or much of a first aid kit. Somehow we jumped Cricket out of the back of the pickup. Mom was using my saddle pad as a blanket or pillow for the girl so we couldn't saddle my horse. Cow camp was closer than riding to Grandma and Grandad's for help so my folks sent me to cow camp, still several miles away, riding bareback. I was upset and remember them telling me that the kids' parents were camped at the Rhubarb Patch and to not stop there but just ride on by. Go to cow camp, tell Bill and Carol what happened and ask them to come help. It felt like the longest ride of my life, especially when I went past the Rhubarb Patch and waved to the happy family who didn't yet know that their kids had been in an accident.

It's funny I remember all of those things in detail but I don't remember anything that happened after I got to cow camp. I imagine we girls stayed at cow camp or someone took us home and the adults handled it. It all turned out okay in the end and the family was grateful for all my folks had done. There was no blame or drama beyond what actually happened. The kids had been taking a ride down to the spring near our upper pasture to get a drink of delicious cold spring water.

≈

Since our lives revolved around horses in one way or another, we girls were always being sent to the pasture to catch horses. Our horse pasture was right up the hill from the house. But the shed where we kept the tack and grain was down the hill and across the creek. So I'd go get a coffee can about half full of grain or rolled oats and a lead rope, then head for the horse pasture. Most of our horses were fairly easy to catch. But if someone else's horse or some of our young horses were in with the others, sometimes it made them all skittish.

The horse pasture was several acres in size so the horses had plenty of space to stay away from us if they got it into their heads to be ornery. The most important thing was to do your best not to spook or chase them. Obviously, horses are much bigger and can run much faster than you can. We knew better than to chase them but sometimes it couldn't be helped. We knew if you get them started running, you're in for a long frustrating time of it. Failure is not an option. No matter how hard it is, you've got to catch that horse. Otherwise, next time they'll remember and be even harder to catch.

My technique was sometimes successful, sometimes not. Always starting on an optimistic note, I stuck the halter and lead rope in my back jeans pocket or looped it around my neck. I'm convinced that with some horses, you really did have to hide the lead rope. With grain in hand, I walked towards the pasture, nonchalantly shaking the grain in the can. Generally, all the horses in the pasture would perk up their ears at that lovely sound. If I was lucky and they were in a good mood, the horses I wanted to catch, and probably all the others, walked or trotted over to me about the time I crawled through the fence into the pasture.

Then, I took a handful of grain out of the can and holding my hand flat, offered it to the horse I wanted to catch. Horses are very gentle when they take something from your hand. If you hold your hand flat, they'll nuzzle the treat softly off your hand. Their whiskers tickle and their muzzle is very soft. Of course, all the other horses crowded in, looking for their own grain. I tried to ignore them and focus only on the one horse until I had the lead rope over her neck. If I couldn't manage that, I'd grab a handful of mane and put my arms around her neck. Either way, though they could have pulled away easily, most of our horses thought they were caught. Then I'd dump a little grain on the ground for the horse I was catching and the rest in several spots nearby for the others. While the horse was occupied with the grain, I'd get the halter over her nose and up over her ears, buckle the chin strap and tie on the lead rope.

But it didn't always work out so nicely. Some horses just wouldn't let you get anywhere near them even with a nice bucket of grain or any other treat (bribe) you might have in your pockets like an apple, a carrot or some sugar cubes. Then you had to catch them by a test of sheer will power. Mostly, will I catch her or won't I? Again, the horse was going to be caught one way or the other even if it took all day to get the job done. I've been known to break into tears of frustration trying to catch a hard-to-catch horse.

Catching a horse that doesn't want to be caught is not really a one person maneuver. So you have to yell for help from a partner. That would be my sister. If one horse took off running, they all ran. So Tammi and I let them run and settle down, then walked towards them, sometimes clear across the pasture. Sometimes more than once. We walked calmly, nonchalantly (yeah, right) towards the horses, trying to move them to a place in the pasture where the fence makes a corner. Sometimes it took some time for the horses to calm down so we walked around with them, waiting. Often we got within a few feet of one of them before they'd all move away. Made me want to just scream. Eventually, we worked them into a corner and one of us managed to get a rope around one of their necks.

Usually, we didn't bother with a halter and just took the lead rope along. Most of our horses led just as well with a lead rope as with a halter anyway. Of course, the lead rope around their neck was always tied with a bowline. For horses that didn't lead so well or were balky for some reason or another, we looped the lead rope over the horse's nose. Then they led better, or at least paid better attention to where you wanted them to go and not dawdling about it.

Most of our horses led like a dream. Once you had the lead rope hooked onto the halter or tied around their neck, they followed along and stopped when you stopped. Other horses just didn't get it. Especially the stopping part. I don't know how many times I've had a horse walk up on the heels of my boots. That was only slightly annoying compared to those horses that just didn't want to be led at all. A brief tug on the lead rope should be enough to get the horse walking. If the horse is still standing there, feet planted, then you have a problem. Common wisdom is you turn the horse in a tight circle, take off walking and they'll come along. That often worked. Pulling steadily on the lead rope, swearing and crying didn't ever help. Eventually you get the horse going, probably by just outlasting them. Then they might lead or you might have a start, balk, stop, start kind of journey all the way to where you were going.

If I had the chance to catch a horse I knew I was going to want to catch later, it didn't matter if I didn't have a lead rope or piece of twine with me. I put one arm up around that horse's neck and hugged tightly, using the other hand to take my belt off and buckle it around their neck. Worked great. Being caught was ten percent real and ninety percent mental especially with an 800 pound animal and an 80 pound girl.

After irrigating was over and there was no water in the ditches, we either let the horses out on the creek bottom or moved them to a pasture with access to the creek. During those summer days, if we kept the horses in the pasture, we had to haul buckets of water up the hill from the creek. We hauled enough buckets of water for the other animals that we had penned up (calves, chickens, ducks, mink, etc) as it was.

When the horses were on the creek bottom, you had to think ahead about which horses you might need or want the next day. They generally wandered in at the end of the day for some grain or a flake of hay. Then the horses you wanted for the next day were caught and put in the corral or the horse pasture over night.

Sometimes we girls took our horses on our adventures. Not wanting to fuss with saddles and bridles, we often rode bareback with a halter and a lead rope. I loved to braid makeshift head stalls and reins out of baling twine. Okay, using twine as a makeshift halter or hackamore depended more on the horse behaving nicely than it did on the twine actually holding if they decided to jerk away. If we wanted to creep along the creek, we'd have to tie off the horses or they'd head for home, so for most of our pretend games and exploring, horses were too much trouble and we left them at home.

Tying a horse to keep it from taking off was a tricky business. There were several things to remember. Giving them a long rope so they could graze was not doing them a kindness. Always tie the horse up short so they can't get their front feet over the rope and get tangled up. Never tie up to a barbed wire fence which could do nasty damage to a horse's chest and legs, as well as tear up the fence. Never tie horses close to each other because no matter how gentle they are, horses in close proximity tend to kick and bite each other and anyone else who got in the way. Also, it was never a good idea to use the bridle reins to tie a horse because they could break or come loose. So if we intended to tie up our horses, we had to carry a lead rope along.

My folks made it clear that they'd rather we didn't tie up our horses at all unless it was to a pole fence rail. When we did, we always used a slip knot which looked like half of a bow. If the tied horse got into some sort of trouble and you had to get them untied fast, all you did was give a quick yank on the trailing end of the lead rope. Some of our horses ground-tied which was very nice. If you had to bail off in a hurry for some reason, all you had to do is drop one rein on the ground. The horse wouldn't move, as if it was tied. Dad had an iron ring buried in the ground in the middle of our corral to teach that concept.

A lot of times we specifically went on horseback rides for fun. Then we usually used a real bridle or hackamore and a saddle. Even if we decided to go fairly early in the day, by the time we got the horses caught and saddled, it was half way through the morning. Mom put lunches in old plastic bread sacks that we tied to the saddle horns and we'd be off. Most of our rides were near the creek so we hardly ever carried drinking water. Sometimes we rolled up a sweatshirt and tied it across the back of the saddle using the leather saddle strings attached to the saddle skirt. In the Colorado mountains, you never know when it might get chilly or rain. When we were little, we usually didn't cross fences because the gates were too hard for us to open and close. But we still had many miles of freedom in which to ride. After all the work it took to catch and saddle the horses and get ready to go, we usually made a full day of it.

My folks were careful with our safety but they weren't smothering and allowed us the freedom to experiment and even take some chances. Sometimes we had some hard learning experiences. The thing is, they taught us how to take care of ourselves and each other and expected us to think things through before acting. Then they had the confidence and courage to let us take some chances and wrong turns in life, as long as we made informed decisions. This was one of those times. If one of our horses came home without us, Mom didn't worry too much. She knew that either the horse dumped us or got untied and we would be walking to the house shortly. Mom and Dad kept us in line with few words and their quiet ways kept drama to a minimum in my childhood.

I considered myself fairly savvy when it came to horses. But I was also an expert at getting bucked off or dumped. This could and did happen any number of ways. If the horse ducked one way to avoid some branches and I wasn't anticipating such a move, I'd hit the dirt on the other side. Or the horse jumped over a stream, ditch or log when I thought they were going to step over it. Or they would shy away at absolutely nothing at all. These quick moves usually took me by surprise and all I could do was grab the saddle horn with both hands and hold on tight. Some horses were better actors than others when it came to shying or spooking. A really good spook had the horse moving its head, shoulders, chest and front legs several feet straight sideways all at the same time. And there sits Kathi on her behind in the dirt again. Finally, sometimes our horses would decide to have their own mini-rodeo and start bucking. Once I was sitting in the dust again, the rodeo was over and we went on about our business.

When I got dumped, most of our horses either headed for the house or more frustrating, wandered around nearby with the reins hanging on the ground just out of reach. Sometimes we'd walk all the way home like that, almost side by side. Don't tell me horses don't have a sense of humor. Sometimes to add the final insult to all this humiliation and bruised ego, the horse stepped on one or both of the reins dragging on the ground and snapped them off. Broken reins were no small thing on our ranch because we didn't have the cash to buy new ones. Daddy did a lot of splicing leather together to repair reins and saddle straps.

The first time I rode Biscuit every spring, we both knew, and so did the rest of my family, that she was going to buck me off. We didn't know when; Biscuit liked to surprise me. But we all knew it was going to happen. She never bucked anyone else off (on purpose) and she never bucked me off again (on purpose) the rest of the summer. Unlike most of our horses, Biscuit then stuck around and let me get up, dust myself off and climb in the saddle with nothing more than a bruised ego and red face.

I vividly remember one particular most embarrassing time like it was yesterday. Several of us were riding horses from Grandma and Grandad's house to ours following the county road. Just as Biscuit stepped off the road, she decided to bunny hop out through the sagebrush. I lasted about ten seconds, then kind of slid onto the ground rather than being dumped in a nice spectacular rodeo-finish. What was worse was I wound up sitting right smack in the middle of my brand new cowboy hat. Talk about adding insult to injury that day.

Even though Dad called most of our horses "knothead" or "SOB" most of the time, he believed horses were smart and many people were stupid and lazy. Bad habits, attitude and behavior in horses were usually caused by bad behavior of people. If a horse had a bad habit, they'd been taught it or allowed to get away with it.

One of the things that made me the craziest was a horse that wouldn't walk but would do something halfway between a walk and a trot that we called jigging. A few minutes of riding a horse like that would be enough to jar your teeth out of your head. Daddy said that such a horse was spoiled or was a dude horse. When my dad called somebody a dude or called a horse a dude horse, it was not a compliment. We had one horse, Vicky, that just wouldn't walk. It was a long ride home, holding her head in, letting up, holding again. Vicky would slow down to a nasty little jig step then speed up to a fast trot and even a full run if you let her until you held her up again. It was annoying and teeth jarring. She turned out to be a better pack horse during hunting season than she was a riding horse.

Some horses wanted to follow another horse so you couldn't ride off alone or take the lead. Others wanted to always be in the lead. And we had several horses that fought you all the way, always wanting to go home. They plodded along all day, barely walking and balking or stopping, nibbling every leaf or tuft of grass they saw and then turn for home if you weren't paying attention. When you finally did head for the house, it was all the rider could do to keep the horse from taking off.

Getting any work done could be a real power struggle. If we were trailing horses to hunting camp or moving cattle and Dad saw one of us fighting with our horse, he yelled at both the girl and the horse. All he had to do was holler, "Who's in charge over there? You or the horse?" and we got motivated to work with our horses instead of working at cross purposes. Don't get me wrong, Dad definitely believed in having a firm approach to dealing with horses. Many times I saw him straighten out a horse and it wasn't always pretty. But if you could get control of the situation and work with your horse without all the drama, that was even better.

≈

On a ranch, the animals always come first. Only after they were groomed, fed, watered, tack put away and horses let out in the pasture could we go finish our other chores and get our own supper. After taking off the tack and putting it in the shed, we brushed and curried the horses while they were eating some grain poured onto a leaf of fresh hay. You never just turned a horse out in the pasture after riding them, especially if they were wet and sweaty, because they could get sick. This is probably where the saying "he looks like he was rode hard and put up wet" comes from. If we'd been doing something on horseback that made the horse sweat, we walked them around a bit until their hair started drying and they got their air back if they were winded.

We had a couple of different kinds of horse brushes. One was wooden with long, soft bristles. We called that the brush. The other was made of coiled metal, the largest about four inches in diameter and had short metal bristles. This was the curry comb and when you used it, you said you had curried your horse. The brush had a leather strap for a handle so you could slip your hand through. The curry comb had a wooden handle, like on a cooking pot. We also had a curry comb that looked more like the brush but was made of stiff rubber.

Most horses loved the attention and I think it felt good to them to get their hair brushed and curried until their coats shined. Besides making their hair lay flat and going in the right direction, brushing helped you get rid of any dirt or mud and stimulated the skin. Most horses loved to have their bellies and chest brushed and they liked having their faces, noses and ears rubbed where the leather of the bridle had been. If that sounds like I'm describing a cat, I guess it's true. Horses can be as affectionate as they can be nasty.

Taking care of your horse's feet is very important to their health and well being. Many horses don't like to have their feet messed with. We spent a lot of time around our horses, practicing, so we could pick up any of their feet and they would stand quietly and get used to having their feet handled. We hardly ever had shod horses on the place because we didn't ride that much on gravel or hard road surfaces. Sometimes the bottom of the horse's foot got packed with mud or got a rock or stick lodged there. You could tell because even though they weren't actually limping, you could sense that something was wrong. So you got off and checked the horse's feet. It was nice to be able to pick up the horse's foot without a fight. Even if she was snippy about letting you pick up her foot, you had to do it. Whatever was causing the irritation had to be found and removed or the horse could easily come up lame. Once the mud or rock was found, you took a stick or blade of your pocket knife, which we never went without, and dug it out, being careful not to injure the soft, tender spot of the foot called the frog.

Dad did a fair amount of horseshoeing, and he was good at it. No hiring a professional farrier for our ranch. We had a big bucket of square-headed horseshoe nails and various sizes of horseshoes in the shed. When I was going to ride my horse, Cricket, in the Fair parade on pavement, Dad wanted her shod. She was a small horse with such a small foot that we had to use mule shoes on her. I think they were size double-ought.

Even without many shod horses on the place, we took a lot of time with foot and hoof care. We had clippers and rasps for that purpose. Think of really big nail clippers and nail files. We checked on the horses hooves every time we were around them. If the hooves got too long, they could impact how the horse stood and walked. Dad clipped the hoof short and as close to the foot as was safe. Then he used the rasp to file off any sharp edges and make the hoof even. He swore that some of our horses enjoyed leaning on him while he was working on their feet. It sure looked that way to me.

Younger horses were a challenge when you handled their feet. They wouldn't lift their foot, wouldn't stand still or, given a chance, kicked whatever was near their back feet. If you were patient and worked with the horse enough, they eventually got used to having their feet picked up. Sometimes, if Dad didn't have time or the colt was just plain ornery, he twitched the horse. The twitch was always a last resort and I remember it only being used a few times when I was a kid. It had a round wooden handle with a loop of cotton rope on one end. Another person (adult) looped the rope over the horse's top lip and twisted just enough to get his attention. While the other guy held the horse that way, Dad then got to work on their feet.

Colts teethe just like human babies do. They love to chew on anything wooden, especially wooden gates and pole fences on corrals. Over the years with lots of colts gnawing on the wood, you'll see gates and corrals that are chewed almost completely through. If one of my folks walked by when a colt was chewing on the fence, they'd tell them, "Hey, get away from there. What do you think you are, a beaver?"

It was a lot of fun watching young horses grow up. They are curious and love to explore the world around them. Just as young people can get themselves into trouble, so can colts. One of the biggest hazards for a colt on the ranch was porcupine quills. We often saw porcupines on the ranch and if there was one anywhere nearby, a colt was going to get into it. Of course, it's a myth that porcupines throw their quills. But if a curious colt, calf or dog sticks their nose near a porcupine for a sniff, those needle-sharp quills come right off the porcupine and get stuck in their nose.

At first, the colt tries to rub the quills away with no luck. The quills work themselves deeper and deeper into the nose and become very painful. We generally saw all of the horses every day but even a single day could get those quills embedded firmly and deep. Porcupine quills aren't that hard to pull out if you can get a good grip on each quill with a pair of pliers and give a good hard yank. The problem is, when a colt is hurting, they're not going to let you catch them very easily or, once caught, stand still and calm to let you pull the quills out. It wasn't easy, but with a lot of time and patience, Mom and Dad were able to get all the quills out each time it happened. Generally, it only happened once to each colt. They quickly learned that lesson.

When you're around any horse, you have to pay attention. It's inevitable that at some point, no matter how careful you are, you'll get kicked, bitten or stepped on. I only got kicked a few times but when I did, they generally got me good and it knocked the wind out of me. They have really good aim and if you're careless enough to walk behind a horse without watching, they'll plant a hoof right in the middle of your chest. You'll find yourself sitting on the ground, gasping for air, wondering what happened. It leaves a nice big bruise in the middle of your chest that lasts all summer.

Whenever we were bitten, it was usually more of a love nip than a bite and didn't break the skin but left a nice purple bruise. I was most often bitten standing next to the horse, facing to the rear and fiddling with the saddle or the stirrup. Just as I was getting my foot in the stirrup and ready to step up, they stretched around and took a nip at whatever part of me they could reach, usually my shoulder or rear-end.

We got stepped on a lot. Horses have great big feet and generally they're shuffling them around rather than standing still. When that big, heavy foot comes down on your toes and instep, it hurts big time. Your leather cowboy boot keeps your foot from being cut or scraped but it doesn't help keep it from getting smashed. Your foot immediately begins to swell up and by the time you get to the house, it's not easy to get your boot off.

Once you got your boot and sock off, Mom had a wash pan ready with Epsom salts dissolved in water from the tea kettle, as hot as you could stand it. There was something very soothing about soaking your foot in the hot Epsom salt water. It seemed to relieve the ache and the swelling both. Of course, being pampered always makes you feel better too.

The same kinds of stickers and burrs that got in our clothes also got entangled in the cat and dog hair and tails. They usually managed to get the burrs out themselves. Burdock grew everywhere along the creek bottom on the ranch. The plant had huge green leaves that smelled when you stepped on them or rubbed up against them. My folks were always waging war on the burdock with a shovel and I think they even used poison a couple of times. But it didn't help much. Cockleburs from the burdock were the worst when it came to tangling in a horse's mane or tail.

It took patience by both the horse and the kid to work out each individual burr. I hated that chore. We usually managed to get them out but sometimes the burrs were so matted, Mom or Daddy had to cut out a section of mane, foretop, tail, or fetlock to get rid of the mess. That was a last resort because it took awhile for the horse hair to grow back and that spot of hair never lay flat or in the right direction again.

Another chore that never ended was pulling tails. Horses need their tail to swat flies. But if it gets too long, it can get tangled, matted and full of burrs, mud and muck. We never cut the hair in a horse's tail. Instead, we pulled it. I kept the horse hair from their tails with a grand plan to braid a wonderful rope or headstall from it. I never did get past a five or six inch braid but it was fun and definitely very pretty. It's best to wear gloves when pulling a horse's tail because horse hair can burn (cause a rash) if it slides quickly between your fingers. Most of our horses didn't mind us pulling their tails. Before long, the tail that had been dragging the ground is short enough to not get tangled but still long enough to flick flies. It's really just a part of a well-cared for horse. A western horse whose tail is neither dragging the ground nor cut straight across looks nice. We were proud that we took good care of our animals and the horses were always neat and well-groomed.

Something we liked to do for fun was to braid the horse's mane and tail. We thought it looked nifty. Dad was okay with it as long as we got it un-braided and brushed out before dark that day. Some of our horses didn't like it at all. But a lot of them stood there and napped in the warm sun while we braided their mane and tail into dozens of tidy braids, neatly all in a row.

Although we branded and earmarked our cattle and we had a special iron for the horses, we never branded them. We made the "lazy H inverted T" brand on our cattle with a straight bar branding iron applied five times. The horse branding iron was much smaller and formed the entire brand on one iron.

Sometimes when you're horseback, especially when you're moving or gathering cows, you can find yourself in a tight spot. If you do get stuck, for instance, facing into a corner between two fences or in a bunch of brush, it's nice if your horse is good at backing. Backing is not a natural movement for a horse. Horses like to see where they're going and can get stubborn when they're in an unfamiliar situation. If they've been taught to back, you pull gently on the reins with equal pressure on each side. Usually you also make clicking noises with your tongue or repeat the word "back". If your horse won't back up, you have to figure out how to get them to turn around in cramped quarters.

When we rode double, we usually did it bareback. Riding double when a horse is saddled is uncomfortable, to say the least, for the person riding in back. Contrary to what you see in the movies, it is not romantic, adventurous or much fun. Some horses simply don't put up well with riders riding double. About the time the rider already in the saddle kicked her foot out of the left stirrup and the other rider got her foot in the stirrup to get on, the horse started sidestepping or kicking their heels up. If the second rider did manage to get a seat on the saddle skirt behind the cantle, they better be hanging on to the person in front or that horse would have them sliding off the rear before they knew what happened.

Another ongoing chore with horses is checking for wood ticks. In the spring especially, and through much of the summer, wood ticks are everywhere in western Colorado. My family said I was a tick-magnet, I got so many stuck in my hairline. Horses also attract ticks where they embed themselves in the skin under the horse's chin and between their hind legs. With the horses, we often didn't notice the ticks until they had been stuck in for a day or so and were engorged with blood. Though it was a gruesome and messy task, for some reason I didn't really mind pulling ticks off the horses. I think it was because the poor horse looked so miserable and I wanted to help make them feel better. Rather than finessing the tick so that you didn't leave their head stuck in like we did when they got stuck in us, we just yanked the tick off the horse. I guess horses aren't susceptible to tick fever like humans are. Then we crushed the tick between two rocks and got another until they were all gone. For that horse on that day anyway.

One time, we had a visit from a college classmate of Mom's and her three kids who were about the same age as us. Of course, all the kids wanted to ride horses. That was fine with our mothers so we all traipsed through the little orchard out front of our house. When we got to the barbed wire fence around the horse pasture, everyone else stayed put while I climbed through the fence. I caught the horse we wanted easily enough. Then, I decided to climb up on the barbed wire fence to get on the horse. I must have been showing off because I certainly knew better.

I climbed up on the fence near a fence post so the barbed wire didn't wiggle so much under my feet. I started to turn around to put my arm over the horse's neck, grab a double handful of her mane and slide on. About that time, a couple of young horses in the pasture who had been milling around nearby started to seriously crowd the horse I wanted to ride. Which made my horse pay more attention to them than to me. In a split second, they all started kicking each other and I ended up on the ground. It wasn't the first or last time that sort of thing happened to me. What made this time different was that I fell between the horse and the fence, apparently falling directly into the barbed wire.

The next thing I remember is the other kids helping me climb back through the fence and heading for the house. There was lots of blood. As was often true of the mishaps we had on the ranch, it could have been a lot worse than it was. I had a few scratches and a single nasty puncture wound where one of the sharp barbed wire tines had put a hole in the left side of my head, near my forehead but in the hair.

Later, Mom said that other people probably would have taken me to the doctor for a few stitches. But as was our "we'll take care of it ourselves" way, Mom got the bleeding to stop, clipped the hair away from the wound and cleaned it out with peroxide. I don't remember how she took care of it until it scabbed over and started to heal but she probably used generous amounts of peroxide, mercurochrome and iodine. Then a bandaid and some sort of ointment (this was pre-Neosporin). After my hair grew back, it was lighter colored. That spot never has lain flat since and was the first of my hair to turn gray. At any rate, all's well that ends well.

No matter how much riding we did or how well we rode, we got saddle sores on the inside of our knees and thighs. Saddle sores are very painful. They feel like a sunburn concentrated in a few spots and there's not much you can do except put up with the pain until your skin toughens up. The worst was in the spring, after not doing much riding in the winter, and it took a few rides to retrain our leg muscles. What's funny is you can ride all day and feel fine. But when you step off the horse, the pain hits. We spent some miserable nights with saddle sores. It seemed like when I had the worst saddle sores was when we'd be riding steady for several days in a row. Oh was it hard to get up that second day and pull those jeans on.

We talked about breaking horses on the ranch and that's what we did. If you said you were breaking such and such a horse, everybody in our part of the country knew what you were talking about. Breaking a horse to ride, neck rein, back, or load wasn't harsh. I guess using the word training rather than breaking might sound more animal-friendly these days but it never occurred to us. At any rate, breaking a horse took lots of time, patience and tender loving care. Naturally, there were curse words and power struggles too but never to the extent that a horse was abused or injured. Yelling at or jerking a horse around was simply counterproductive. My dad believed that horses remembered things like that and would never work with or for you again.

Sometimes we didn't have the luxury of time to completely break a young horse so Dad had to speed up the process a bit. That's why he ended up riding green-broke horses a lot of the time. The rest of breaking that horse was mostly on the job training. We always got the job done when we were moving or gathering cattle. But it did provide some comic relief for the rest of us when one of the green-broke horses Dad was riding decided they'd had enough and suddenly started bucking out across the pasture or out through the brush.

Sometimes my dad, uncles and their friends had an impromptu, informal rodeo in the corral at our house. They would get one of the young horses and manage to get him saddled. Or they would use Dad's bareback rigging from when he used to ride the rodeo circuit. While everyone else sat on the top rail of the corral, one person held the horse's head while someone else tried to mount up. The person who'd been holding the horse would run for the fence. Then it was a matter of who could stay on the longest with extra points for style, whatever that might mean. Nobody got hurt except maybe for some bruises and banged up ribs. Everybody had a lot of fun, participants and spectators alike.

Horses sleep standing up but they love to lie down and soak up the sun to get warm. Anytime there was a cold or wet night and the Colorado sun came out bright the next day, it was common to look out in the pasture and see several of the horses lying flat out on their sides, soaking up as much of the warm sun as possible.

In the early mornings or evenings around dusk, sometimes all the horses in the pasture took off running together. Often when a storm was brewing and there was a cool, brisk breeze, one horse would prick up their ears and take off "like a bat out of hell" across the field, all the other horses close on the leader's heels. They might run like that for a long time. It was a lot of fun to watch, especially when Biscuit was part of the bunch. She always held her head high but when she was running, she had both her head and tail up and was just beautiful. Dad said it was because she was part Arabian. You can't help but be happy, watching them run and play like that.

Hunting Season   13

Hunting season was a very big deal at our house. As licensed big game guide and outfitters, my folks not only guided the hunter to the deer or elk but also outfitted them with tent, camp gear, food and pack horses. We spent a lot of each summer in the mountains for fun and while we were at it, we scouted out where the game was. Then, for a couple of weeks before hunting season, Mom and Dad got camp all set up and ready for the hunters. Even though it meant long days and hard work, my folks loved taking hunters out. They didn't do it just for the money, although that was good. The lifestyle appealed to them, that frontier, pioneering spirit and it fit right in with the life we had on the ranch.

My family knew the mountains and loved being there. We loved the country and the wildlife. Ranchers, who make their living off the land, are the original conservationists, coexisting in a healthy way with all nature's inhabitants. Taking hunters out was a good way to share that message with city folk, give them a good hunt and make some money in the process.

Through the Guide and Outfitters Association and by word of mouth, hunters contacted Mom and Dad. After coming the first time, many of our hunters came back year after year. As the years went by, Dad's reputation grew and he had more hunters inquire than we had space in camp. My folks booked as many hunters as they could handle for the two hunting seasons, elk and mule deer, in the fall. The hunters were all dudes in our eyes, from Texas or Oklahoma or somewhere else far away. They had big fancy guns, more money than they knew what to do with and no common sense.

Mom and Dad handled all of hunting camp by themselves. Sometimes Uncle Ernie or Luther helped trailing horses to camp, guiding, and packing meat back to camp. A big part of hunting season happened during the weeks before season actually started.

During hunting season, we girls still had to go to school so we stayed with Grandma and Grandad Arthur. I think it was two weeks for elk season. I'm not sure about deer season, which was earlier in the fall. It was a treat to stay with Grandma and Grandad. They always treated us as if we were special. One of the best things was the indoor bathroom and hot and cold running water! We ate and slept at their house and they got us to and from the school bus stop.

We hung out with them while they did the chores although I don't think we were much help. They worked on the ranch all day and every morning and evening, the milking had to be done. After evening chores and milking were done, we had supper and sometimes watched TV if there was anything on that Grandma and Grandad wanted to watch. If there wasn't anything on TV, we played cards, usually pinochle. It made us feel so grown up. Or else we watched Grandma and Grandad play cribbage. I don't remember learning to play either pinochle or cribbage, just learned it from watching.

Bedtime was early and we never thought to challenge it no matter how much we didn't like it. We grew up to respect our elders and that included no back talk. That's just the way it was. There wasn't much time for reading in bed before Grandma turned the lights out and I didn't even think about trying to read under the covers with a flashlight like I did at home sometimes. In the morning, she often woke us with a warm washcloth on our faces.

One night we asked Grandma if we could fix supper. She said yes. She had a roast in the oven. All of our meals on the ranch revolved around what meat we were having. So that part was done. While Grandma and Grandad went to milk and do chores, we peeled potatoes and put them on to boil. We cooked green beans and made a green salad. We felt very grown up and thought we were being such a big help.

We set the table and got the bread out. Everything went fine until we mashed the potatoes. We'd watched and helped Mom and both Grandmas do it hundreds of times and it seemed so easy. Just add butter, salt and pepper and milk and keep mashing with the potato masher until there weren't any more lumps. We didn't have any lumps in our mashed potatoes that night. But we added so much milk that our mashed potatoes had the consistency of the roast gravy Grandma made when she got up to the house from chores. Tammi and I felt miserable. To Grandma and Grandad's credit, they complimented us heartily on how good the supper was and said the mashed potatoes were just fine.

Grandma and Grandad left a lamp on in the living room during hunting season. When I was a kid, no one left any lights on and we'd never even heard of a nightlight that you left plugged in. We all had flashlights handy because when it was dark, it was very dark. There were no streetlights and no glowing from electronic gadgets. Just dark. So it was odd sleeping in a house where a light was left on. Even though the light was downstairs and a long way from where we slept, the house wasn't dark like we were used to. Apparently some road-hunter had shot towards the house, more than once, so Grandad left the light on during hunting season to remind road-hunters we were there.

Lots of things set my dad off but I've never seen Dad and Grandad more upset than when they were talking about road hunters. First of all, it was illegal to hunt from the county road. But that's not what got Daddy's Irish up. It was a whole series of things. To him, and a lot of other ranchers, I imagine, road hunters were worse than dudes because they were careless, lazy and dangerous. Then there was everything else. You never carried a loaded gun in the vehicle. You never shot from your vehicle. These guys were shooting at deer or elk on private property. There were cows and horses out in some of those fields. There was a house with people in it on the other side of the fields. All in all, a very bad deal. Once someone shot one of our mules and another time, they killed a bull (Hereford, not elk).

Another time, Dad got some revenge. It was in the evening and we were all at Grandma and Grandad's house. Someone went up the road in a pickup, driving slow. Suddenly there was shooting from the road up above the Thirteen Acres. Dad and Grandad jumped in the pickup and took off "like a bat out of hell." Soon, the hunters went down the road with our pickup not far behind. They kept going toward town when Dad turned into Grandma and Grandad's lane.

After telling us briefly what happened, Dad got back in the pickup, headed up to the Thirteen Acres and soon came back to the house with the hunter's rifle he found in the field. When Dad and Grandad first went up the road, they found the hunters pickup stopped in the middle of the road. Dad confronted the road hunters and reminded them that shooting from the road was illegal. I'm sure he was very pleasant and tactful. Well, maybe not. One of the hunters protested. My dad took his rifle away from him and threw it out into the hayfield. He told the hunter he'd be trespassing if he went to get his gun and they should turn around and head back to town. I think Daddy also threatened something about the game warden. That's all I know. And thus was born another favorite family story that was told, retold and embellished over the years. But I was there when it happened!

≈

The most critical thing about hunting camp was its location. We spent a lot of time in the high country in late summer and early fall during the elk rutting season. Dad figured out their migration patterns, where they watered and grazed and where they bedded down. That's where camp would be. Often Dad picked the location for hunting camp so well we used the same camp site for several years. On these outings, while we all sat still and quiet at the edge of a high country meadow, Dad used an elk bugle to whistle in a bull elk. He was skilled at it and we would hear the elk bugling back to him long before we saw it enter the meadow. The sound of an elk bugling in the distance is amazing. It's not something you can describe; you've got to be there. And they were so beautiful when we first spotted them at the edge of the meadow, head held high, huge rack of antlers back so far they were almost touching the bull's back. One of Dad's elk bugles was made of hollowed antler and the other was of bamboo. They were handmade.

One summer, our big project was taking a big old iron cook stove to hunting camp. You couldn't drive to this particular camp so everything had to be packed in. We drove way up in the mountains and took off out through a meadow where there was no road. Dad stopped the pickup near the top of a very steep hill. I'm sure he drove as close to camp as he could get. My folks had built a slip much like that we used for haying. It was a little bigger than the stove, made of two poles set a few feet apart and covered with a plank floor.

Somehow Mom, Dad, Grandma and Grandad Arthur got the stove out of the bed of the pickup and onto the slip. They tied the stove down then slipped it down a steep hill, through some spruce trees and into camp. Nobody got hurt and nothing got broken though on a couple of steep places, I think it was touch and go whether the whole load was going to get away from them and go flying down the slope.

I'm not sure who first had the idea for the cookshack. I think Mom described what she wanted and Dad figured out how to build it. It was brilliant and Mom loved it. The four sides were made of plywood, hinged together so the whole shack folded up and fit in the bottom of the pickup bed. It was big enough for the stove, a table and benches for eating and playing cards, and a living quarters for Mom and Dad tucked in one corner. The cookshack was much more airtight than the old canvas army tent they used before so it was quite warm. A clear visquine plastic roof let in sunlight during the day.

Even with the cook stove and shack, camp was mobile. We just left the stove in the trees near camp from year to year. Back then, we knew if someone happened to stumble upon our gear, they would neither steal nor vandalize it. So Mom's life was much easier because she had a full size wood burning cook stove, a set of box springs to sleep on and a cookshack with plywood walls and a heavy plastic roof.

We spent several weekends before hunting season cutting, hauling and stacking firewood. We also set up the cookshack and the heavy canvas army tents where the hunters would sleep. We were expected to be good help and we were, but we also made it fun. Dad used a chain saw to cut up dead spruce and quaky trees near camp. We all had a hand in carrying and stacking the wood in neat stacks near the tents and cookshack. Often this was during the World Series so we'd have the radio on in the pickup and if you were close enough, you could hear the baseball game.

After camp was all set up and there was plenty of firewood, there was still lots to do to get ready for hunting season. Groceries would be bought, horses and hay moved to camp, and hunters retrieved from the airport in Grand Junction. Since we had no phone, Mom did lots of letter writing, corresponding back and forth with the hunters to make all the arrangements for their arrival.

Buying groceries for hunting camp was a big adventure for us. Mom made sure we were out of school when she shopped so we could help. We went to City Market in Rifle where we did our regular shopping for the ranch. This was heavy duty shopping. Among other things, we bought lots of canned vegetables and fruit, huge bags of potatoes, onions, flour and sugar, rolls of toilet paper, bags of apples and oranges, boxes of candy bars, dozens of eggs and many pounds of bacon, coffee, lard and butter.

Mom made all the bread, cakes and other desserts from scratch at camp and Dad provided an elk or deer for camp meat. She made the cookies at home, ahead of time. Still, our shopping trip involved three, sometimes four, loaded shopping carts and several hundred dollars. Two or three hundred dollars was a fortune to us. It also bought a whole lot of groceries in those days. When Mom filled up a shopping cart, we left it parked somewhere in the store. When she was done shopping, we helped her gather up the carts and get in line to check out. Getting that many groceries was as much of an event for the checkers and baggers as it was for us. All those groceries and all that money was a world of plenty, even excess, that we only saw once a year, getting ready for hunting season. When we were done shopping, the pickup bed was packed full of boxes and paper sacks.

When we got home, I think Mom did as much sorting and repacking as she could while the groceries were in the back of the pickup to save unloading and reloading. Over several days, all the groceries and other supplies for two weeks in hunting camp were loaded into the back of the pickup and hauled to camp. For lighting in camp, they used kerosene lanterns so we had lanterns, wicks and fuel to take. We had to haul in hay, grain and all the tack for the horses. Mom was an excellent organizer and I'm sure she had many lists. As the years passed, Mom and Dad learned what worked and what didn't. Between them, they thought of everything and planned so they had enough of everything they needed but not so much they would have to haul a lot back home after hunting season.

≈

A few days before opening day, we trailed the horses to camp and got to take off school to help. The last few years my folks did guiding, hunting camp was way over on Thompson Creek, south of Glenwood. This was a two day trip with the horses. Trailing horses to camp included the horses we rode and the other horses that would be used as pack animals. If you've never hunted with my dad, you might be surprised to learn that hunting involves lots of walking and sitting and very little horseback riding. After hunting on foot, if you shot something, then you used a horse or horses to pack the game back to camp.

Many of our horses were barely green-broke so trailing horses to camp wasn't necessarily as simple or straight forward as any old trail ride. Early in the day there was usually some excitement while riders and young horses vied for control and got comfortable with each other. As the day wore on and we got further from the ranch, horses and riders settled into somewhat of a routine.

Sometimes we had to lead horses that wouldn't stay with the rest of us going up a trail or out through the trees. Leading a horse while on horseback is a tricky business. Some horses just wouldn't do it. The biggest problem was the two horses picking at each other, kicking, biting, snarling and generally annoying each other and all the other horses and riders. As the rider, you just tried to stay on your horse, keep hold of the lead rope, keep the lead rope out from under your horse's tail (very important) and hope they behaved without the shenanigans that can happen when horses get too close to each other. Most of our route to hunting camp was out through the timber. So another hazard when leading a horse is that horse going around a tree on the other side from where you and your horse went. We managed to get the job done with only a few minor entanglements.

Sometimes the horses that weren't being led or ridden decided to go off in the trees on their own. If one went, they all went. Usually they didn't go far. When they noticed that we were leaving them behind, they'd hurry to catch up. Once in awhile they just kept wandering or even took off, headed for home. When that happened, things could get exciting for a little while. Dad told us to stay put with whatever horses were still with us and he and Uncle Ernie took off on their horses to round up the wanderers. Sitting and waiting for them to come back sometimes felt like a very long time. Eventually we'd all get back together again and continue on our way.

The first day of the ride was quite a bit shorter than the second day because Dad made arrangements with another rancher, Mr. Sherwood, to leave our horses in his high country corral overnight. It was right beside the road and Mom met us there with hay and grain for the horses and snacks for us. Once the horses were watered at the creek and settled in the corral, we went back to our house for the night.

The next day was long and mostly cross country with very few roads. We dressed appropriately, fully expecting to be wet and cold when we got into camp. We took our usual lunches in old bread sacks, just lots more of it: a couple or three sandwiches, several apples or oranges, a big bag of cookies, some potato chips and a pocket full of candy bars. We didn't carry anything to drink. When we were thirsty, we drank from the creeks we passed along the way. Dad, Luther (a friend of Dad's) and Uncle Ernie usually had some bourbon along to help them keep warm..

From Sherwood's corral, we stayed on the road and went on up past East Divide Cow Camp to just below Willow Creek where we left the road and headed up a gully. Now we were going as much east as south towards some pretty big mountains. Those mountains separated the Divide Creek drainage from the Thompson Creek area. We had to go over, around and through them.

We rode mostly through trees on narrow game trails, single file, following the tops of ridges when possible to avoid steep hillsides and slide areas. We rode around peaks and through gaps between higher mountains. We often followed a creek, then for no reason known to us, Dad would veer off from the creek out through the trees again. He seemed to have his own personal built-in GPS. We never saw another person except those in our group. We girls knew how to keep quiet and stay alert in the mountains with the reward of seeing whatever critters we might encounter. We saw deer, elk, weasels, porcupines and sometimes a beaver when we rode by beaver dams. If we were lucky, we saw bald eagles, wild turkeys and sage hen. There were lots of squirrels, chipmunks, cotton tails, woodchucks and birds. It was cool and quiet, just the sound the horses made walking on branches and the creaking of leather.

We went around Big and Little Baldy and when we saw Haystack Mountain actually below us (it was a pretty tall mountain), we knew we were almost to Haystack Gate and Baylor Park. Riding through Baylor Park, we felt like we were almost to camp. We had come a long way but still had quite a way to go, mostly uphill. We rode past a whole string of beaver dams in the creek and then the ruins of one of President Teddy Roosevelt's bear hunting cabins, then hit the Four Mile Road. A highlight of our day was to check the forest service sign that said "Baylor Park" for messages. If Mom had already gone by in the pickup, she left us a message tacked to the sign and a bag full of treats. If we got there first, Dad left a message for her. It was getting on towards dusk and starting to get cold by the time we left the Baylor Park sign and headed south.

Before long, we took off cross country again. Right before we left the road, it rounded a huge curve. One year, Luther was riding with us on either Little Joe or Thunder.

The horse took off around the corner and kept going faster and faster. Luther started to lean off to the side, then he was really leaning off to the side, then he was flat on his face in the cold, icy creek below the road. When we saw he wasn't hurt except for a few bruises and his ego, we all thought it was hilarious. Especially since we knew adult beverages were involved. Since Luther was soaking wet, Dad didn't waste any time hauling him out of the creek, getting us all mounted and headed for camp again.

Another time, someone who was with us caught up with Dad on the ride. He asked Dad if he knew that girl back there (me) was riding and reading a book at the same time. Didn't surprise Dad in the least.

By now, we were all cold and wet, it was starting to get dark and trailing horses to hunting camp wasn't all that much fun anymore. We hunkered down in our coats, hats and gloves and toughed it out. We were sure happy to see the light from Mom's campfire and kerosene lantern when we topped that last hill before camp. When we got to camp, we hurried to unsaddle and brush down the horses. Once they were fed and tended to, we ran for the cookshack where Mom always had steaming hot homemade chili and hot chocolate waiting for us. Pure heaven!

≈

During hunting season, when a hunter got something down, they gutted it out on the spot and hot-footed it back to camp. Dad, Uncle Ernie or Luther helped get a couple of horses geared up with pack saddles and panniers and saddled up a couple of horses to ride. I'm sure they didn't waste any time getting headed back out of camp because they didn't want to chance a bear, wildcat, lynx, coyote or turkey buzzard getting into the meat.

Pack saddles were made of sturdy boards, maybe 2 x 4s, that crossed each other in the front and back making a structure that looked something like a miniature sawhorse. The ends of the crossed boards were made to loop ropes around and hold such things as panniers. Our panniers were big heavy duty canvas bags with sturdy leather handles on each side. The seams were both stitched and riveted. When the handles were hung over the pack saddle on an average sized quarter horse, the bottom of the bag hung below the horse's belly. Packing a horse took some attention to detail or you could end up with a spur of the moment rodeo with the horse kicking, squealing, bucking and eventually tearing up your pack saddle and panniers. The most important thing about packing a horse was to get the balance and weight right.

Depending on the size of the deer or elk, a horse could pack out two quarters or all four quarters. For an average sized buck, you might put a front and hind quarter in the pannier on each side and pack out the whole deer on one horse. Not so with a bull elk which is much bigger than even the biggest buck. It would take a pretty hefty quarter horse to haul a whole bull elk at one time. If the hunter wanted the head to have it mounted at a taxidermist, they pack it, otherwise Dad just packed out the antlers, attached to each other by part of the skull. After packing the meat in the panniers and making sure that the horse wasn't ready to pitch a fit, they put the antlers on top and tied off the whole load. Usually, the antlers were carried by tipping the antlers upside down so that the skull portion sat in the center of the pack saddle and one antler hung down on each side of the pack horse, tips pointing toward the ground.

Dad got a deer or elk, probably not on any license, for Mom to use as camp meat. The best part of a deer or elk is the backstrap. It is the most tasty and tender part of the meat and it's about the only part of the animal, besides the heart, that we cooked and ate right after the animal was dressed out. Wild game needs to age several days before it's at its best for eating.

Whenever a hunter got something, they'd bring the deer or elk heart back to camp for Mom to fry for supper. The liver is good too; I know because both Grandma Cole and Grandma Arthur told me so. After trying it once, I'll take their word for it. None of our family could stand the smell, taste or sight of the stuff even though we all knew it was good for you. Thankfully, for our sakes, Mom felt the same way as the rest of us did about liver so I'm pretty sure she didn't cook much liver at hunting camp either. At home, when Dad got us meat out of one of our hayfields (farmer's season), Mom sometimes cut up the liver for the cats and they loved it. But usually the liver went the way of the rest of the deer or elk "innards."

≈

Most years when we set up camp it was late-fall weather and not much snow, if any, on the road. Out in the dark timber there might be several inches but days were warm enough so any snow out in the open where the sun hit would melt. By the end of hunting season, conditions could be considerably different.

The road wasn't maintained and to get there if there was much snow or mud, we spent the last several miles in granny gear, four wheel low, chained up all the way around, grinding through the mud and the snow. We gained several hundred feet of elevation in those last few miles so you were always going up steep grades and around sharp corners.

Most of this part of the trip was through black timber. There were lots of big tall spruce, quakie and pine trees packed closely together. The sun didn't break through very much, if at all. Every stretch of road was either steep and slick, or if it got enough sun to melt a bit, there were a whole series of mud holes to contend with. Mom and Dad were both very good drivers on very bad roads. I was notoriously a bit of a worry wart. Mom said I got that from Grandma Arthur. But no matter how much I didn't like the trip, the destination was worth it so I rode it out. If Mom or Dad were driving, I had absolutely no doubt that everything was going to be just fine. And it always was.

When we got to the end of the road, we drove another really difficult half mile or so on to camp. It was lava flows and a huge boggy marsh. Our whole part of the country was volcanic and we had plenty of granite, basalt, quartz and other neat rocks and minerals. We were all rock hounds. One of the most fascinating things was the lava flows. The country might look like everything around it, steep, tall hills, lots of trees, rocks and rock outcroppings, when suddenly you came upon a lava flow. It seemed like all the dirt disappeared and there was nothing but hundreds of boulders, all about the size of a washing machine or a television, for as far as you could see up the mountain. The rocks were stacked one on the other, I don't know how deep.

Nobody even attempted to build a road through the lava flows. If there was a road, it stopped at one edge of the rocks and started up again on the other side which could be several hundred feet or more away. All you could do was pick a route across the lava flow that looked good to you and start driving across it, your tires bouncing from one rock to the next. Sometimes a rock turned over or slid, so the tire slid and the pickup lurched, making for a little excitement.

That's what we ran into up Thompson Creek where the road ended. The first time we drove that way, I thought my dad was nuts but he said the camp site was just around the next corner. Where there was no road. Sometimes that was the only way he could keep us going when we got tired or discouraged was to tell us "it's just around the next corner", or, "it's just over the next hill."

In this case, not only did we have a huge lava flow to cross but the whole beautiful little valley was one huge marsh. It was green and grassy when you looked at it. Pretty and serene, the creek meandered through the middle of the meadow, like a postcard or poem. If you took many steps into it, it felt mushy under your foot. A few more steps, the ground got wetter and mushier and suddenly it seemed like it was trying to suck your foot under. Driving in it, or on it, was very tricky. Talk about getting stuck. But it took so long to get across the lava flow in places and some of it was too steep to even try. So Dad decided to find a way to make a road across the marsh. He walked ahead of the pickup and pointed. Mom drove where he pointed. This was the same technique we used out in the trees where there was a mud hole we just couldn't get through and had to find a way around. Turning around and going back was never an option with my family.

Even though the pickup sunk in, it didn't break through and we actually drove across it and back several times. A couple of times, the pickup broke through into the muck and we were stuck. I have no idea how we ever got out. A couple of years later, we moved hunting camp back to the other side of the bog and lava flow.

We all loved that camp site. The creek was down over the hill so it wasn't that big of a deal to carry buckets of cold, fresh water up to camp. There was a nice big stand of spruce, pine and quakie trees that provided plenty of shelter from blizzards that were inevitable during hunting season. We could drive the pickup right to it, usually anyway. We hauled the cook stove into camp in the back of the pickup, and had plenty of room to set up Mom's cookshack and the tents for the hunters. There was room for us to build a little corral between the trees for the horses. And there were lots of dead trees nearby to cut up for firewood. There was also a great big patch of gooseberry bushes that we watched all summer and picked when they were plump, juicy, sweet and still green, not quite ripe. Green gooseberries make the best jam.

One year there was a huge blizzard that dumped many feet of snow in the high country. The tents were set up, hay hauled in and most of the cooking supplies already at camp. Trying to get into camp, my folks could only get about as far as Park Creek, pushing more than three feet of snow with the pickup. While they were trying to figure out what to do, they met a guy who worked for Rocky Mountain Natural Gas. He was up Four Mile checking gauges on natural gas wells and had a snow cat. They got to talking, as country folk will do, and Dad told him their predicament. Using the snow cat, the nice young man took my folks on into camp.

The old canvas Army tents had split right down the middle from the weight of the snow. With hunters coming, they had to set up camp somewhere. With the snow cat, they moved camp down to Park Creek and borrowed tents from everybody they could think of. The hunters who had already arrived helped them set up a new hunting camp. Arbaney's ran a sawmill down Four Mile and sent their son with some kind of big machine. He cleared the road from the top of the hill down to Park Creek.

During the summer, we drove to hunting camp from the ranch by going up West Divide Creek or East Divide Creek. For much of the year, those roads were impassable. They were really just jeep trails to begin with. So even though we brought the horses to hunting camp cross-country from the ranch, everything else was brought in the long way around by going from the ranch to Silt, on to Glenwood and up Four Mile, past Sunlight Ski Area. The ski area was as far as the road was maintained by the county.

Above the ski area, the road climbed steeply up the side of the hill and went past a big, deserted sawmill. It looked like it must have been quite an operation in its day. At the sawmill, the valley opened into a big high country pasture.

Across the creek, was an old cabin where Martin Lyke lived. He was kind of rough looking and reminded me of a mountain man. Besides the cabin down by the creek, there were several ruins of old buildings. I think it may have been a coal town as well.

Usually when we referred to hunting camp, we just said "camp." Once camp was setup, we girls were out of the picture because we had to go to school. But I've heard Mom, Dad, Luther, Uncle Ernie and some of the hunters tell enough stories enough times to get a picture of how things went at camp. On weekends and if school was out, someone came and got us and took us to camp.

Hunters were one or two to a tent with their own little campstove for heat and kerosene lantern for light in each tent. They were old army tents made of heavy dark green canvas and were surprisingly airtight, warm and roomy enough for their sleeping bags, hunting gear and other belongings.

Mom and Dad had their own tent until the cookshack was built. One corner of the cookshack held a set of box springs set up on logs, with their pillows and bedroll which they liked better than sleeping bags. There was the cook stove and a table and benches for eating, playing cards or whatever.

Mom did all of the camp work by herself. It was hard work and she was good at it. She started early, long before daylight. There was always a big breakfast of fried or scrambled eggs, bacon and fried potatoes along with a skillet full of pancakes, French toast or biscuits with pots and pots of camp coffee. She also made sack lunches for the hunters before they left camp to go hunting.

Big game beds down during the middle of the day so the best times to hunt are at dawn and dusk. From all the scouting we did, Dad knew where they might be moving so that's where he put a hunter. Once they found a good spot, the hunter hunkered down, waited and watched.

After everyone was out hunting, Mom had camp to herself. Well, she should have had. But I think there was often a straggler who didn't go out because they were ill or some other excuse. Or they stayed to help. Mom wasn't a complainer but after hunting season we often heard lots of animated stories from Mom about her helpers at camp. At home, I know Mom had trouble getting us to help without always reminding us to do things over and over again. Many times she said it was easier and quicker to do it herself. Another saying, from Aunt Mary I think, was "if you can't help, don't hinder." It sounds like those hunters who stayed in camp to help Mom were a combination of the two sayings in the worst way. Anything they did to help made the job go twice as long or Mom had to redo the whole thing anyway. If they weren't already in camp, they came at the first smell of baking bread.

If the hunters or guides needed something that wasn't in camp, Mom had to go to town or all the way to the ranch to get it. That would kill the whole day, especially if the roads were bad. Luckily, that didn't happen often because Mom was good at planning ahead. One time, she had to go to town for something and a hunter decided to go along to keep her company and help. His help consisted of him staying in the cab of the pickup and giving Mom advice through the open window, telling her how to put on the chains so they could get through a mudhole. If I were her, I would have left my helper sitting alongside the road, talking to himself.

Mom made dozens of cookies at home ahead of time for lunches. We didn't have chocolate chip cookies at home very often because chocolate chips were expensive. Same thing at hunting camp. But Mom had lots of other yummy cookie recipes. One of the most popular with we kids and hunters alike was hermits;

Hermits

- Mix 1 c soft shortening, 2 c packed brown sugar, 2 eggs.
- Add and stir in ½ c cold strong coffee.
- Sift and stir in 3 ½ c flour, 1 tsp cinnamon.
- Mix in 2 ½ c raisins, 1 ¼ c chopped nuts.
- Chill at least an hour. Drop by spoon onto greased pans. 400 degrees. 8-10 minutes.

Besides the cookies, she baked everything else in that old cook stove at camp. She made several loaves of bread every day and cake, cupcakes or cobbler almost every day.

The creek wasn't far from camp, just down a little hill. It wasn't a big creek but it ran fast and fresh. Mom dug out a hole in the creek deep enough to dip a bucket and come up with a full one of fresh, cold water. They used the creek water for drinking, washing up, and doing dishes. Hauling water and chopping kindling for the stoves took some time. Then it was time to get supper going. Supper was simple but nutritious, tasty and there was plenty of it. Meat, potatoes, vegetables, fruit and dessert. I imagine sometime during the day, Mom found the time to just enjoy being in the mountains, read a book, or write a letter.

If someone got game there was a flurry of activity getting the meat packed into camp. No matter how many hunters got something, it was always exciting. In the evening, there would be poker playing, lots of tall stories about today's hunt, and plenty of drinking. Dad made it very clear to the hunters that liquor and guns don't mix. But there was plenty of partying in camp at night.

Just as we never had loaded guns in the house or pickup, there were no loaded guns in camp either. Hunters learned first thing, if they didn't already know it, to load their guns only after they'd left the area of the tents and other people. Just outside of camp, they sometimes set up paper plate targets or aluminum cans for target practice. If the hunter had a new gun or Dad suspected they didn't have much experience, they sighted in their rifles. Life at camp revolved around tall tales and guns. It was hunting camp after all.

Post Season   14

After hunting season, the hunters were all returned to
their cars or put on planes in Grand Junction and sent
home. Camp came down a lot quicker than it went up. On
the day Mom and Dad took down camp, first thing in the
morning we turned all the horses loose. It may have taken
us two days to get the horses up to hunting camp but they
sure didn't need any help or that much time getting back to
the ranch. At first, they were a little unsure about what to
do but after a little whooping and hollering and some
enthusiastic slaps on their rear ends, those horses that
knew the routine and had done it before took off for home
with all the other horses right behind them.

Then we spent the day taking down tents and packing
the pickup full of camp stoves, tents, lanterns, saddles and
other tack, and all the other gear that needed to be hauled
home. If there was room, they took any leftover firewood
home. Otherwise, we restacked it back in the trees   for

next year's picnics and camping in the summer or hunting season in the fall. They buried the trash, common practice in those days, filled in the camp outhouse hole and took down the corral. They took the plastic roof off the cookshack, folded up the walls of the cookshack and packed it in the pickup, then stowed the cook stove back in the trees. We always left a neat campsite whether we were there for two weeks, a couple of days or just a few hours for fishing and picnicking.

While my folks were taking camp down, we girls looked through the straw that was on the ground in the cookshack under where the table had been. Dad said we could keep anything we found. We often found a treasure trove of loose change, especially quarters. Over the years during the poker games at camp, my mom ended up with a nice twenty-two pistol and a beautiful turquoise and silver belt buckle. She didn't participate in the games so someone either gave them to her or Daddy won them. Besides the quarters, we picked up pockets full of spent shells from just outside of camp. We kept the twenty-two shells to take home and play with. All the other empty casings we gathered up for Dad to take home and reload.

We never worried about the horses. There were only a few fences between camp and the ranch and the gates were open this time of year. They didn't waste any time making the trip and either beat us home or showed up shortly after we got there.

One year, there was a lot of early snow in the high country. We turned the horses loose for home as usual. They didn't show up. After a couple of days, Dad got in touch with a friend of his who had a plane and they flew the area where the horses should be. They found them in a mountain meadow all settled in where the snow wasn't as deep and grass was still sticking up through the snow. The next day, Dad and Uncle Ernie rode other horses up into the high country to head them home again.

≈

We cut up and packaged our own deer and elk meat. That's how our family had always done it. It was more economical to do it ourselves but the main reason was because we all thought that the way we did it made the meat taste better.

We boned out the entire deer or elk and cut off every piece of fat and gristle. Mom and Dad said those are partly to blame for making wild meat taste and smell strong and gamy. Locker plants processed deer and elk the same way they did a beef. They used their electric meat saw and cut right through the bone, dragging the bone marrow into the meat. In beef, that adds to the flavor. In wild meat, it makes it taste strong.

We cut everything into steaks, stew meat or hamburger. We never cut deer or elk roasts because we preferred it fried. We used the meat pounder on the deer or elk steaks, dipped the pieces in milk soured with a little vinegar, and rolled them in bread crumbs. Then Mom fried them to a golden brown in hot lard in an iron skillet. On hot summer days, she used the electric frying pan. She always cooked plenty and leftovers were always gone by bedtime. Deer or elk steak cooked that way also makes the most delicious gravy.

Another clue to making deer or elk taste their best is the aging. As soon the animal was killed, Dad cut off the head, gutted it and hung it upside down to let the blood and liquids drain out of the chest cavity as quickly as possible. The sooner you put the meat in a cool place, the better. It didn't take long out in the hot sun for meat to spoil. Aging the meat for at least a week, if possible, made it more tender and tastier. We hung the meat in the shed behind our coal shed or in Grandma Cole's root cellar in town.

Dad left the hide on the meat while it was aging to help keep it from drying out. If that wasn't practical, Mom made canvas meat sacks. These were better than store-bought ones made of a porous material like muslin which lets the air get to the meat and dries it out. About the only good use for those meat sacks was to keep the meat clean and keep the flies off.

Cutting up deer or elk was an event at our house. We had a system where everybody knew what they're job was and we were all good at it. When we were cutting up meat, we used the kitchen table, the dining room table and at least one card table. The day before, Dad sharpened his favorite hunting knives and Mom's kitchen knives. Grandma Cole helped and sometimes brought long-time friend, Martha Terrell. Mom called Martha her "second mother" and we girls thought of her as "big Martha."

Dad quartered and skinned the carcass and brought in one quarter at a time. He worked in the kitchen. He had a special meat saw and hatchet we knew weren't ever used for anything else. They were sharp and clean and helped get the game carcass into a manageable size before he started deboning. Hind quarters had more meat on them but front quarters took about as long to get it all deboned.

We first checked for hair stuck to the meat and used a damp rag to pull the hair and any dirt off the meat. Then we looked for bloodshot through the meat which was bad meat caused by bruising from the impact of the bullet. Those sections of meat, if any, were cut out and thrown away. The dogs and cats got their fair share of bones and meat when we were cutting up an elk or a deer.

Once Dad had the meat off the bone, he put it in big chunks in a pile on the freezer paper we used to cover and protect all the tables. We did all the trimming and wrapping in the living room where there was more room. We used all of Mom's cookie sheets and cake pans to hold and move meat during the process. Now we decided what was steak, stew or hamburger. To us, the decision was made by whether you could get some "nice sized" steaks off the chunk of meat or not. We loved our deer and elk steaks so anything bigger than about three or so inches wide and long was considered steak-size.

To get a nice, tender steak, you wanted to slice the steaks against the grain of the meat. It would be tough and stringy if you cut it with the grain. With practice, you learned how to tell which way the grain goes. It looks much like the grain in a piece of wood. We sliced the steaks about a quarter of an inch thick and if we couldn't figure out how to slice a particular chunk of meat against the grain for steaks, we chunked it up for stew meat. The steaks were tossed neatly on a cookie sheet or some other pan where another person started trimming. Leaving fat on beef brings out the flavor. Leaving fat on deer or elk makes it taste strong and gamy.

If it wasn't a steak, we figured out whether it was stew or hamburger. If it looked like a piece of stew meat, then that's what it was. Otherwise, it went into the pile to be ground for hamburger. (okay, deer burger). It depended on whether Mom needed more stew meat, more hamburger, or equal amounts at that particular time. We wrapped all the meat, whether steak, stew meat or hamburger in amounts about right for a family of four. If we needed more for a meal, we just opened more packages. We also wrapped much smaller packages for Grandma Cole because she lived alone.

The meat was centered on the shiny side of the freezer paper nearer one corner than the other three. We got very good at folding the corner and rolling the package, securing the flap with a strip of masking tape. With a black marker, we wrote the contents on the paper, using abbreviations. "D Stew" or "E Stk" or D Hamb" would do. We got good at making neat, flat packages of meat as pretty as birthday presents about six by eight inches. They stacked nicely in the freezer.

My folks and grandparents were all great about not stressing over things and keeping drama to a minimum. They saw what needed to be done, then did it. With sharp knives and an experienced crew, cutting up a deer or elk goes smoothly. At the end of the day, we were all tired but as Mom says, it was a "good" tired. And best of all, we had meat in the freezer.

Mom's kitchen knives and Daddy's hunting knives were always sharp. Daddy kept his whetstone handy and many evenings I remember him sharpening knives. He was quick about it and when he sharpened knives, Mom said they stayed sharp longer than when anyone else sharpened her knives.

We girls took great pride in helping with trimming and wrapping meat, even when we were too little to handle a knife. Our original job was to cut the freezer paper to just the right size and tear off strips of masking tape which we stuck all around the edges of the card table where Grandma Cole was wrapping. Our goal was to keep a steady supply of paper and tape so the people doing the wrapping never had to stop and wait or get their own.

While trimming and wrapping was still going on, Dad finished boning, took the carcasses and scraps out of the house and did some clean up. Then he and Mom clamped the big meat grinder onto the edge of the table or counter in the kitchen and started grinding hamburger. When Mom knew we were going to be cutting up deer or elk in the next few days she got several pounds of beef suet at City Market. If City Market didn't have enough, she got it at one of the locker plants in Rifle or Silt.

Running all that meat and suet through the meat grinder was hard work and made your arm real tired real fast from cranking the handle. My dad was always one for finding an easier way so he took a small electric motor from an old wringer washer and hooked that up to the meat grinder with a rubber belt (like the fan belt in a car). Now you just had to feed the meat and suet into the grinder and wipe the outside of the blades from time to time. When the hamburger clogged up the holes in the blade too much, they stopped, unscrewed the ring that held the blade in place, cleaned as much meat and fat out of the holes in the blade as possible and put it all back together again. Washing the grinder took lots of hot, soapy water.

Meanwhile, wrapping continued. We single wrapped (one sheet of freezer paper) unless we thought the meat would have to be frozen a long time (several months) before it was cooked, then we double wrapped. That meant wrapping the meat once, turning the wrapped package a quarter turn and wrapping it again on another piece of freezer paper. This gave the meat double protection from the drying conditions in the freezer and kept more air out so the meat could stay frozen longer without freezer burn.

"Many hands make quick work" is an old saying that was definitely true at our house. Mom, Dad, Grandma Cole and we two kids could put up a lot of deer or elk meat in one day. It was hard work but we had a good time with visiting and talking going on all day.

Mom bought freezer paper on a great big roll from the locker plant. There was one in Silt (Gross was the family name) and two in Rifle. A locker plant processed and packaged meat if someone bought a beef, pig or sheep. They also processed wild game and packaged it with dry ice to transport for out of state hunters. There were lockers in a great big walk-in freezer that could be rented. Mom rented a locker several times when we had too much deer and/or elk meat for our freezer.

We processed and packaged our deer and elk as usual, then took the packages to town in cardboard boxes. Mr. Gross stamped each package with our last name and put it in our locker. The lockers were a series of wooden cubbyholes built around the walls of the walk-in freezer. They had a door in the front of each locker made of a wood frame and chicken wire so you could see what was in the locker. Then when Mom had room in our freezer, we'd stop at the locker on our way home from town and get a box of meat. Even though they were called lockers and had a latch where you could put a padlock, I don't think Mom locked our locker. It was a time when people trusted each other. No one would even think of taking something that wasn't theirs.

Over the fireplace in our living room was a huge set of elk antlers. My Dad had killed the elk and mounted the impressive antlers. Among other things, we used it as a gun rack and hat rack. We had other antlers on the wall in the living room and probably would have had more on the walls if our house was bigger.

When Dad got an elk or a deer, there wasn't much wasted. We ate the meat and pulled the eye teeth for Mom. Generally, the hunters wanted the antlers as their trophy and let Dad pop out the eye teeth. On an old bull elk, the eye teeth were big and looked like aged ivory. In fact, we usually called them the ivories. The teeth were rounded and worn smooth because of the age of the bull and the dark spot or "eye" was a deep brown. Dad made beautiful earrings for Mom and other friends and relatives from them.

During hunting season, we took deer and elk hides to town for the Boy Scouts to collect as a money making project. We kept the antlers, including the portion of the skull where the antlers were attached. Dad cut a shield shape from a piece of plywood, mounted the antlers and finished the project by covering the skull part with green or red velvet fabric and gold upholstery tacks. Almost everyone we knew had at least one set of Dad's antlers hanging in their house and they thought it was something special. We usually had several sets of antlers down in the shed that needed to be mounted.

Counting the number of points on a set of antlers can be done several different ways. Our way was by the side with the fewest points. So if there were six points on one side and five on the other, we called it a 5-point. A point has to be at least 2 inches long to be counted so the brow points over the animal's eyebrows usually couldn't be counted unless it was an older animal. Dad said if you could hang a ring on it, it counted. As antlers were shed in the fall and grown again in the spring each year, and as the animal aged, the antlers were bigger and had more points than the previous year.

Besides the number of points, the dimensions (width and height) of the antlers were important as well. The goal was bragging rights and to get your picture with the antlers into the Boone and Crockett records. The elk in our country could get really big. Over the years, we had some antlers that were so big, it was all the pack horse could carry. They were tied upside down on the pack saddle and the tips were almost dragging on the ground.

We said "horns" when we meant "antlers." Everybody we knew, except dudes and city folk, called them horns. We knew they weren't the same thing and we knew the difference. I know I got annoyed when somebody thought they were going to teach me something and explain the difference between horns and antlers. They're probably the same people who never missed a chance to tell us that creek is pronounced "creak," not "crick." Well, sometimes when I was playing down by the crick I found deer horns that had been shed. So there.

Every year in the spring, deer and elk shed their antlers to grow new ones so we were always on the lookout for antlers on the ground. Like losing a baby tooth, the new antler literally pushed the old one off. Whenever we were out on the ranch, in the woods, or in the mountains, we looked for those antlers that had been shed. We called it "picking up horns." The younger generation calls it "looking for sheds" these days. Grandad Cole had picked up horns from decades of being out in the mountains. He had a stack of deer and elk horns that was taller than me stacked around their yard-light pole in New Castle.

When the antlers were close to coming off, deer and elk liked to rub their heads up against a tree trunk or bush. Mom said getting new horns must itch. Usually, we only found one horn at a time but sometimes, rarely, we found a matched set, the individual antlers having been shed in the same general vicinity. When we found antlers, we took our prize home to show Mom and Dad.

Trap Lines and Raising Mink 15

In the winter, Daddy worked with the Colorado Game and Fish Department to trap beaver and lynx cats from East Divide Creek and the surrounding area. Dad got a bundle of long, skinny, shiny aluminum tags that were tied together with a string from Marion Lowery, the game warden living in Rifle. They were attached to each pelt before shipping.

Sometimes Dad got permits for West Divide Creek as well if the beaver were causing a problem building too many dams over there. One year, we trapped several beaver out of West Divide Creek on the Philpott place. They had a huge house built of stone. It was fun to go to their place with Dad because they had lots of peacocks. We liked to watch them spread their feathers and then lay them flat again. We found several peacock feathers we took home to play with.

I suppose the number of tags allotted to my dad was based on population trends of the lynx and beaver, and how many he thought he could trap in a season. We had tags for trapping a specified number of beaver and a specified number of lynx each winter. Though it wasn't his intent, sometimes Dad caught rabbits, muskrats and other small critters in his traps.

Grandad Cole had been a big trapper and hunter for many years so my dad learned a lot from him and I think most of the traps Daddy used had originally belonged to Grandad. So were the snow shoes he used to run the trap line.

Both beaver and lynx were plentiful in the creek bottoms and on the hillsides around the ranch. On any of our treks up country, we would see one or two lynx. It wasn't as common to see a beaver out and about because they're fairly nocturnal and did most of their work in the evening and after dark. One of the many reasons it was so neat to live on the ranch and go to the high country was all the wildlife we saw. We never took it for granted and never got tired of spotting critters and stopping to watch them.

Most years, the beaver had the creek dammed in so many places you couldn't count. Beaver dams often interfered with ditch headgates. I happened to like beaver dams because they were great for fishing. I don't know if it proves out, but Daddy said if there were more beaver dams than usual, the beaver were trying to save water because it was going to be very dry next year.

A lynx is related to but not the same animal as a bobcat although the two are commonly confused. Bobcats have a tail and are darker in color than a lynx. A lynx has a short stub of a tail beautiful light brown to gray spots, and very distinctive tufts of hair on the tips of its ears. Even though we knew better, sometimes our family referred to lynx as bobcats. Or we simply called them "cats."

Dad ran his trap line just as the old timers had, either on foot or on snowshoes. I thought of Dad's trap line as a path he took along the creek, partially using deer or livestock trails, from trap to trap. He often covered many miles in a day checking traps. The trap line could stay the same for much of the winter trapping season or it could change from day to day. It all depended on where Daddy was catching beaver or lynx. If he caught a beaver, he might move the trap, or he might leave it there if he thought there was another beaver working in that same dam. It all depended on where the animals were.

Trapping was a winter time activity so it could be very cold and wet with deep snow to break through to keep a trail open between where the traps were set. This was not a job for the faint hearted or weak willed. After a few years, Dad had the opportunity to buy a snow machine which helped make traveling the trap line and hauling animals back to the house easier. Even with a nice packed trail, it took quite a bit of busting through the snow on foot to get from the snow machine to where the traps were set.

Dad carried his traps, bits of rope or baling twine and whatever he might need to run his trap line that day in a gunny sack. Gunny sacks were burlap bags that livestock feed and seed for planting fields came in. They were strong and durable, and just the right size for lots of ranch chores.

The lynx traps were set on the hillside, not too far from the creek. Getting to the traps sometimes meant scrambling through brush, up and down steep, slippery creek banks. In the middle of winter, you had deep snow to deal with. Snowshoes work great, up to a point. But in tight places, where you're almost crawling through the bushes and sliding down the hill, they just won't work.

Our snowshoes were made long before they made the modern short, light, metal frames with metal spikes for gripping that are sold now. They had wooden frames and animal gut strung across the frame in a webbing, sort of like a really big tennis racket. There was a leather strap to hold the toe of your winter boot in the snowshoe. One pair of our snowshoes were very long, taller than I was when I stuck one end in the snow and the other up in the air. They weren't much wider than the boot. The others were shorter and fatter. Both sets were heavy and clumsy, and it took practice to use them effectively. Once Dad had a path packed in the snow, he didn't have to wear the snowshoes as much as he did right after a fresh, deep snow.

When he got something in a trap, Dad tied a rope to it and carried it over his shoulder. If it was a beaver, he drug it behind him in the snow. They're very heavy. If he got more than one animal, he might have to make more than one trip back to the house.

He had a really old, heavy, khaki colored parka that he wore only for trapping. I think it may have originally been an Army coat. Dad liked it because it was warm and had lots of big pockets. To me, it was greasy, grimy and smelly because he carried at least one bottle of cat "scent" in one of the pockets. I don't know if Mom ever washed that coat or if he even brought it to the house. He may have left it at the shed. If he did bring it to the house, I'm sure it hung on the porch. Besides his heavy coat and a gunny sack, Dad had a knife in a scabbard on his belt and a 22 pistol.

One day, Mom and Dad got the chance to buy an old snow machine. That changed things for the whole family. We got it to make working the trap line easier but we also used it for hauling things, pulling sleds and just having fun. The snow machine was a Ski-doo brand, big and yellow. Unlike the sleek, light weight, fast machines that Uncle Ernie had, ours was heavy, wouldn't travel very fast, and was slow to turn. If the smaller machine got stuck in the snow, even a kid could lift, shove and eventually get it unstuck. With our SkiDoo, two kids couldn't budge it.

Our SkiDoo was a double track. It had two tracks and two skis instead of the one track and one ski on the other snow machines. The advantage was that it made our SkiDoo more stable, less likely to turn over and much stronger to chug through the snow pulling a load. Dad used the SkiDoo to break trail in the snow for his trap line and he could carry everything he needed with him and haul anything he trapped back to the house.

The trap line ran from our house, quite a distance on up the creek. Lynx and beaver were trapped roughly along the same trap line, but with different traps and techniques.

From years of working the ranch and noticing things around them, my folks knew where lynx territory was and could spot likely locations for den openings under rocks, dirt overhangs or the dense underbrush that was common on hillsides near the creek. When a den was found, that's where Dad set and scented the trap. For lynx, Dad used a trap much like you read about or saw in stories about frontiersmen. The traps were quite small; you don't want a bear trap to catch a cat. Setting the trap took great care because you could easily get caught and seriously injured.

The scent we used on the traps was homemade from different oils and liquids of the animals Dad trapped and hunted, and smelled terrible. I didn't ask many questions because I really didn't want to know. The scent was stored in small glass spice or pill bottles with tight screw-on lids. It served its purpose well in attracting the lynx.

When the catch for the day was hauled home, the animals had to be skinned or pelted out. Some days there weren't any cats caught and other days there might be one or more. A lynx was skinned without making a long cut in the hide. The result was a tube-like pelt, shaped much the same way it had been when it was on the animal. If done properly, the only holes in the pelt were where the tail and legs were, the eyes, nose and mouth.

Next, the pelt was turned inside out so the hair was on the inside. Using a very sharp knife, the inside of the pelt was fleshed out. Old fashioned straight razors were better than knives. Any meat and fat remaining from the skinning were cut/scraped from the pelt. This was tricky because you wanted to get as close to the skin as possible without putting a hole in it. It took years of experience, and a very sharp knife or straight razor, to get skilled at fleshing out a hide so it would dry.

Once the hide was fleshed, it was turned inside out so the hair was on the outside. Then the hide was pulled onto a stretcher. Just like the traps, we got the stretchers from Grandad Cole who had designed and made them. Mom always said "necessity is the mother of invention." The fleshing and stretching had to be done the same day the cat was skinned, before the hide began to dry and stiffen up. As with many of the best tools on the ranch, the stretchers were simple and efficient. They were made of 1 x 4s, about six feet long and curved at the end for the head and nose of the pelt.

We tagged the hide with the permit from the Game and Fish and leaned the stretchers against a wall or hung them on bridge spikes on an outside wall of the house. Once the pelt was completely dry, and consequently very stiff, it was pulled off the stretcher. The pelt was kept for shipping at the end of the winter and the stretcher was used again on another hide. I think the same stretcher was used for coyotes though Dad wasn't big on hunting coyotes. Coyotes weren't a problem around our ranch and pelts weren't worth anything.

Once, Dad found a young cat that had been orphaned so he brought it home as a pet. Somehow, he managed to get the lynx out of the trap and tied into a gunny sack. He had been thinking about getting a lynx for a pet for awhile so built an escape-proof cage out of chicken wire in our back yard. Every hole in the chicken wire, and all the places where the wire had been cut to shape the cage and wired back together was no more than 1 ½ to 2 inches wide.

Dad managed to get the young cat out of the gunny sack and into the cage. He always said wild cats were easier to catch than they were to turn loose. This may be where he came up with that saying. We stayed clear of the cage because the cat was all snarling teeth and long, sharp claws. He could reach his front leg a long ways out through the chicken wire if you got too close and he was much quicker than we were. We spent a day or two watching the lynx, feeding it, talking to it, thinking that with persistence, we could tame it into a nice pet. The next morning, the cat was gone. The best we could tell was it had bent a portion of the cage so there was a hole through the wire just 3 or 4 inches wide and got out that way.

This experience reminded us of something we already knew; wild animals are not meant to be tamed and made into house pets.

We used conibear traps for beaver. They were made of heavy steel bars about a foot or so square and spring loaded. They were set partially in the water, near beaver dens in the creek bank or beaver slides. These traps were even harder and more dangerous to set than other types and it took a strong person to get the job done.

As with the lynx, Daddy hauled the beaver to the house and skinned them. This time a slit up the middle was appropriate as the final result was a perfectly round pelt. The beaver was skinned and the hide stretched. The beaver stretcher was a homemade board made of thick plywood, cut about five foot square. We laid it flat on the floor and the beaver hide was placed in the middle of the board, hair side down. Centering the hide on the board, two very small nails were nailed through the very edge of the hide and into the board opposite each other. Then two more nails were added opposite each other so there were four nails, forming a square. You wanted the opposite nails to be far enough apart so the hide would be stretched tight when you finished. But if you got the hide too tight with those first few nails, you wouldn't be able to pull the last of the hide out far enough without tearing it to get a round result. If the hide was too loose with the first few nails, it would still be too loose when you finished. Nails were added in the same way until the hide was perfectly round, stretched taut and had nails about every quarter inch around the circumference. It took a lot of practice to get really good at stretching a beaver hide.

Finally, the hide was fleshed out and left to dry on the board. Taking care with the entire process made the pelt worth more in the end. Fleshing out the beaver hide took patience and as usual, a sharp knife or straight razor. With the hide stretched so tight, it was very easy to cut a hole in it. I watched my dad flesh out beaver pelts for many hours over the course of many years. He held the blade almost flat against the hide and made short, slicing strokes. As the bits of fat and meat came off the hide, they stuck to the blade. Dad kept a warm, wet rag handy and wiped the blade often. We girls helped stretch and flesh out the hides to earn spending money. The nails made holes in the hide but they were very small and very close to the edge of the pelt. When the hide was dry, the nails were carefully removed and the pelt stored with the lynx and other beaver pelts to be shipped in the spring.

A weasel is a long, skinny animal with a long tail and short legs. When we got our mink, I thought they looked like a weasel. The first time I saw a pet ferret, I though they looked like a weasel too. Weasels were pretty, brownish red in summer, and then they turned white in winter. When they were white, their pelts were called "ermine" which was very much sought after. But it was still a weasel. Weasels were elusive and we didn't see them very often.

Some years, Dad had trap lines far up in the high country above the ranch. These years, we sometimes caught weasels. One time, we caught a pine marten. They were rare, even in the high mountains. The marten seemed a little like a weasel but much bigger. Apparently the fur was rare too because Dad made almost as much money on that one pelt as he did all the beaver and lynx pelts combined that winter.

Any small hole or slit accidentally cut in the hide lowered the value of the pelt. Animal hair dulls a knife faster than anything. So Dad always had several knives sharpened and, depending upon how many animals he was skinning and fleshing out, he might have to stop in the middle of the job and sharpen all the knives again. Many of Dad's knives had been handmade by Grandad Cole and those were the ones he liked the best because they kept an edge, or stayed sharper longer.

All of the skinning was done outside the house. Mom put up with a lot in her house but either she drew the line at that one or else Dad didn't ask. Stretching and fleshing out of the lynx hides was done outside. Fleshing out and stretching a beaver hide seemed trickier, took longer and was more delicate work than it was with a lynx so we did that in the living room after supper on winter evenings.

Dad loaded carcasses from hunting and trapping into the back of the pickup and hauled them up-country, to some gulch away from the house where predators and nature took its course.

At the end of the trapping season, all of the lynx and beaver pelts were bundled in gunny sacks and shipped off to the buyer. The gunny sacks were torn or cut open at the seams, then stitched together with string and a big needle normally used for stitching with leather to form larger bags for the pelts. It wasn't a lot, but the cash from selling the pelts was money that belonged to Mom and Dad, not part of the ranch funds, and we depended on that money every winter.

≈

One time, Daddy and Uncle Steve decided to raise mink for their pelts. Since they lived in town, we would keep the mink at our place. Prices paid for the pelts were based on color, quality and whatever the market could stand ie. what was the fad of the year. This was before furs became politically incorrect. Everyone with money wanted a fur coat, stoll or collar. Living as close to Aspen and other haunts of rich people as we did, raising mink sounded like it would be quite the little money making proposition. Things don't always work out that way.

Mink were beautiful but nasty little animals. They were white, black or various shades of brown. They were long necked, with a long slim body, long tail and short legs. With their perky little ears and long nose, they looked much like a ferret or weasel. Mink looked so cute and harmless. Contrary to their appearance, they had lots of sharp teeth and were extremely ferocious. Dad was the only one that handled the mink and he bought special thick leather horsehide gloves that went to his elbow for the purpose. The mink were kept in wire cages. We were warned over and over to not get our hands anywhere near the cages. We learned why when my sister put her hand flat against the side of the cage one time and had four perfect (and painful) pricks on her palm where the teeth had gone around the wire and into the palm of her hand.

We had hundreds of mink, each in its own cage that Dad, Mom, Uncle Steve and Aunt Nancy built. They were made of wire with ¼" squares cut out of big rolls of wire, shaped, bent and fastened to make the cages. They were about 18 inches wide by 1 ft tall by 2 ft long and sat on wooden benches that we also built. Row after row after row of them. The cages were in mink sheds – some of the sheds had already existed on the place, others were built for the purpose. It took my parents a lot of time and hard work to get ready for the mink.

The mink were delivered from Utah and each got its own cage. That's when the work really began. Feeding those critters was a full time job for Mom. We fed them ground up meat with who knows what else in it. It was messy and smelly. Sometimes Uncle Ralph caught suckers in the river and Mom ground up the fish, bones, guts and all. The grinder was made with a washing machine motor and an old hand meat grinder using a pulley. Because of the sheer volume of feed we needed, we usually bought it from a large mink farm in Delta. When we needed mink feed, we went to Delta and got a pickup load, a 2 ½ hour trip each way.

The feed was spread in flat cardboard boxes (like what soda cans used to sit in on the grocery shelves). The feed in the box was frozen solid. We loaded the boxes of feed into the back of the pickup, covered it with a tarp and headed for home. The quicker we got home, the quicker we'd get those mink feed boxes back in the freezer. Thawing mink feed was messy and smelly.

I don't know why we weren't using our own pickup but the summer we went to Delta so often to get mink feed, we used Grandad's old pickup. When I was a kid, it had never been used before. It just sat in the corner of Grandad and Grandma's driveway and we kids played in it. I don't know what Dad had to do to get the thing running again, or when he got it a nice shiny new coat of bright red paint.

The truck was a 1948 GMC with a wooden bed and stock rack. It also had a hole in the radiator. We carried several old Clorox jugs full of water with us. Every time we came to a creek or river, we pulled over, let the engine cool off, filled up the radiator and refilled the jugs. Then we continued on our way. It took us a long time to get to Delta and a long time to get home (with the feed seriously starting to thaw) but somehow Mom made a game out of it for us and I remember how much fun we had on those trips.

Every day, Mom got the mink feed out of the freezer to thaw. She dumped the thawed feed into a great big metal dishpan which she tucked under her arm. Then she put a very large spoonful of the glop on top of the cages. Besides feeding, cages had to be cleaned and replenished with fresh straw, so that involved some logistical headaches in terms of moving the mink around.

When the mink were bred. Dad moved females in and out of the cages with the males. When the young were born, they were in litters of four to six. They were about the size of your little finger, hairless and very pink. They were actually kind of ugly. We were used to playing with all the animals on the ranch. Looking at (but no touching) the mink wasn't all that interesting, so after awhile we went somewhere else to play.

Once a year, the mink were pelted and the pelts sold. We girls avoided the mink sheds when it was going on. When my folks realized how much work the mink were at very little profit, they got rid of them all and we didn't raise mink any longer.

The End

Contact Information:

Please feel free to contact me at:

KathleenArthur@hughes.net

Enjoy!

Kathi

CPSIA information can be obtained at www.ICGtesting.com
Printed in the USA
LVOW101723270613

340559LV00020B/810/P